MARKETING STRAIGHT TO THE HEART

Marketing Straight to the Heart

Barry Feig

AMACOM

American Management Association

New York • Atlanta • Boston • Chicago • Kansas City • San Francisco • Washington, D.C.
Brussels • Mexico City • Tokyo • Toronto

Library of Congress Cataloging-in-Publication Data

Feig, Barry.
     Marketing straight to the heart / Barry Feig.
        p.   cm.
     Includes index.
     ISBN 0-8144-0355-7
     1. Brand choice. 2. Motivation research (Marketing)
  3. Marketing—Psychological aspects.   I. Title.
  HF5415.3.F393   1997
  658.8—dc21   96–52678
                                        CIP

Printing number

10 9 8 7 6 5 4 3 2

To the people who love me
and whom I love in return—
and especially to my children,
Meredith and *Jeremy*,
who are MY hot buttons

Contents

Preface

The most captivating moments in any Olympic games are not in the athletic endeavors—most runners and swimmers look pretty much the same while performing—but what happens after the event. The emotions of the achievers, winning or losing, often transcend the actual accomplishments.

This book is about emotions and achievements—marketing achievements.

You can't separate the selling of a product, any product, from the emotions that come with buying that product. That's why successful companies, even companies with such unglamorous products as tires, base their marketing strategies on emotion. Those Michelin commercials featuring babies are a great deal more effective than just listing dull factoids and factory specs. People who sell time-shares and vacation properties spend a great deal of time learning about their customers' emotional wants and needs before they show the property they are hawking. They sell a dream rather than reality.

Emotion is critical to every phase of business, from product planning and development to marketing to R&D. It should be built into every marketing plan. Even when one pitches an idea to management and stockholders, it's necessary to push the correct emotional buttons as well as to talk about numbers and potential markets.

This book is based on interviews and work I've done with consumers and the companies that sell to them. When I say consumers, I include businesspeople. I've spoken to a great many people over the years in both consumer and business-to-business market segments, and this book is the outgrowth.

The tools for achieving marketing success are spread throughout the book, but I suggest you read Chapters 1 to 3 as a complete unit, for they are the foundations of the book.

A basic premise is that whether one appears to be selling a product or a service, one is really selling a service—the ability to do something or provide something for someone else.

Marketing is not a science, despite the proliferation of business books and technobabble that would have you believe differently. Marketing is a learned, applied analysis of human behavior. This book does not in any way pretend to be scientific. But the methods have been tested and proven time and time again.

—Barry Feig
newmex@aol.com

Acknowledgments

There are a great many things that go into the making of a book. All of the work I've done for clients over the years have helped me learn the importance of marketing "to the heart."

I would especially like to thank my acquisitions editor, Adrienne Hickey, who, in her own unique business style, helped me craft the book so that it met with our vision. Mike Sivilli, my associate editor, juggled temperaments and egos (I have no idea how) so that the final product met our common goals.

I also like to thank my friends and loved ones, who so patiently read my original drafts and trashed them so skillfully and diligently.

Thanks to all.

MARKETING STRAIGHT TO THE HEART

▶ 1

What Is Share of Heart? How Can It Work for You?

It was a big day for this particular American business. The decision was a decade in the making. Workers fought about the move, both in boardrooms and in after-work taverns. The CEO of the company, one of the most prestigious in the world, had the final say, and he would not hesitate to vote down the move. He knew that the decision affected millions. He did not take his responsibility lightly.

When the decision to make "the change" was announced, it made news on all the major networks and in almost every big-city newspaper. The change affected almost everyone, from two-year-olds to grandparents—no matter what their vocation, race, or sex.

Was it a new type of computer?

Nope.

Was Ford introducing a new prototype vehicle?

Not a chance.

I'll give you a hint. It was blue, about half the size of a penny, and—oh, yes—it melted in your mouth, not in your hand.

Yes, the blue M&M's made marketing history. This is especially fun when you consider that blue M&M's taste the same as the late lamented tan ones they replaced, which tasted the same as the red ones, which tasted the same as the yellow ones. And blue isn't even considered a good color for food.

Why all the fuss? Why did it take Mars years to make what seemed like an ordinary, and sound, business decision?

Because Mars knew that when it tinkered with its product, it tinkered with our most important part—our heart. Mars knew that M&M's were a part of our growing-up experience. They were an emotional tie to the past.

Win the hearts of consumers and their minds will follow.

Marketing success starts with the heart. The supreme challenge is not merely to market a better product but to build into your marketing plan a message that speaks to consumers on a personal, emotional level.

You're not sure how strong the pull of emotion is? Than flash back to a memory you have of an important moment in your past. It could be something from your youth—a memory from college or high school, or even from before you entered your teens.

You're probably flashing back to an emotional moment. You might have laughed. You might have cried. But you remember that moment above all others because it triggered an emotion in you. The emotional pull was so strong that this event overcame in your memory the millions of other events that have made up your life to this point. It may have had no great impact on your life, but you still remember it as if it happened a few minutes ago.

Behind every number on a spreadsheet is a living, breathing human being who wants to be dazzled by a product or service. But you see, there's a problem. These people are skeptical. Who can blame them? They see new products and new pitches come and go every day. They have heard every marketing spiel. Your potential customers get up in the morning and are accosted by ads on their cereal box. They fall asleep to the perverse lullaby of infomercials about the latest abs-blast machine.

But even in the jumble of pitches and products, people will react to the product that says, "I know who you are. I know what you want."

The pull of emotion. The power of the heart. It's a power that we as marketers can harness. A product that triggers emotion is a product that will be remembered. Learn the hearts of your customers and you can build brands and businesses.

Consumers won't admit it, and most often they don't even realize it, but the heart overrules the head in almost every purchase decision almost every time. Can you buy affection? Yes.

The Importance of the Emotional Hook

Vest your product with emotional interest and you can have a winner in the marketplace. The good taste or performance can last six seconds or less, but the good feeling it provides can last a long, long time.

Here are some examples.

The alcoholic beverage industry learned long ago the power of the emotional sell in the product. In the liquor business, a "call" brand should look and sound good when being requested (as well as taste good).

Why? Because consumers want to feel special for being smart enough or cool enough to order it. A short time ago, Seagram's marketers decided that they were in the luxury, fashion, and entertainment businesses, not the booze business. So they jettisoned a whole host of brands that they felt no longer emitted a luxury aura. The real profits were in the premium prices they could charge for brands with well-developed emotional strengths.

Pet food producers and baby food producers have (or should have) learned a special marketing trick: big eyes. The most effective packages in this category feature babies and puppies with eyes that are wide, large, and open. There's something in our genetic programming that makes big eyes effective and irresistible. Want proof? Check out any Steven Spielberg movie. The eyes of the good guys, usually aliens, are large and vapid, while those of his villains, e.g., the shark in *Jaws* and the monstrous creations for *Jurassic Park*, are all tiny.

What's pink and white and cleans your toilet? Why, it's Toilet Duck. S.C. Johnson wanted to enter the toilet-bowl cleaning market. It could have competed by using a tough-sounding name like Bully or Vanish. Instead, it went a different route and added an element of fun to the product. Although cleaning the toilet will never rival sex or Nintendo for good times, using a product called

Toilet Duck with a funny-looking neck on the bottle does liven up (for a moment anyway) the worst job in the house.

In service industries, the best sales- or account people do much more than sell business services. They create relationships. Just being skilled in a specific area or trade is not enough. An important facet of the job is understanding your customers so that you can relate to them on a personal level. One owner of a successful midsize business fired her highly respected accounting firm not because of the quality of the work or the price, but because the accountant intimidated her. He made her feel embarrassed because she did not understand number juggling or the intricacies of the tax laws. Smart service marketers bond with customers. They make them feel comfortable and gain their trust.

This is especially important in a downsizing environment. If a manager decides to take you on and buy your product, one of his or her first thoughts may be, "I hope this guy doesn't get me fired. I hope he or she makes my boss appreciate me." There are many, many insecure managers out there. It's safer not to hire a new supplier because a nondecision is easier to explain to management than a wrong decision. You have to reinforce the fact that you're on the manager's side and that you're going to make her or him look good. These people are usually buying trust and security as much as the actual goods and services.

Share of Heart

I call this emotional involvement with a customer the product's Share of Heart.

Share of Heart is how consumers respond to your product emotionally, as opposed to intellectually. It's the connection you make with your consumers—an emotional state in which the consumers respond through feelings, rather than through cold, hard facts. It's where you put all the elements of your product together and create a product that's more than the sum of its parts.

You achieve Share of Heart when you infuse your product with something of great emotional and personal value to the individual consumer. It's the vital right-brained message you send to consumers that causes them to make a commitment to your product. Share of Heart is how consumers perceive that your product relates to their needs. This all-important aspect is the one you can't photograph, but can control.

Share of Heart answers the two key questions that are part of almost every purchase: (1) How is this product going to "reach out and touch" the respondent, and (2) how is it going to improve the buyer's life? It's about adding a touch of salesmanship to your product through subtle cues.

Despite what a great deal of research suggests, consumers want to believe your product works. Share of Heart gives them a basis for believing.

The power of the heart is universal, transcending geopolitical and cultural boundaries. In China, which likes to consider itself the most egalitarian of countries, there was a black market for counterfeit labels of the most prestigious bicycle manufacturer. People wanted to show off their new "top of the line" bike as we like to show off our Mercedes.

The power of the heart is why America cared when M&M's brought out its blue candy.

In the over-the-counter drug business, unique, to-the-heart positionings have allowed manufacturers to remain extremely profitable despite the straitjacket of stringent FTC regulations and the strategic bombardment of private-label knockoffs. TheraFlu, from Sandoz, is an excellent example. TheraFlu is a cold medicine that is meant to be taken hot and at night. It's sort of like a 1990s update of chicken soup. Although there's no scientific proof that TheraFlu works better than room-temperature cold concoctions or tablets made with the same ingredients, the imagery is strong and unique. Mothers can relate to the steamy hot ingredients soothing a cold away. By appealing to the emotions, TheraFlu's astute marketers have parlayed this simple product into a business that threatens NyQuil—the first on the block with a nighttime cold medicine.

Share of Heart for Continuous and Continuing Sales

You can't create an ongoing business on one sale. It's how the product performs after the sale that determines repeat business. The selling venues may vary, but to be successful, a product must be sold four times.

In a retail situation:

1. On the shelf
2. At the checkout counter
3. In use
4. After it runs out

In a service situation:

1. When you walk in the door and make your presentation
2. After your presentation
3. When your product or service is used
4. After the product or service is used

In a direct mail situation:

1. On the first page of your mailing or catalog (or magazine ad), or even on the envelope
2. In the response mechanism
3. When they get the product
4. When you're ready to sell to them again

Share of Heart in One-Shot Sales

In some circumstances, you have only one opportunity to sell. This occurs in certain direct sales of products that a customer does not buy frequently, such as real estate and other large-ticket items, and in telemarketing pitches and infomercials. To be totally crass, this is called the take-the-money-and-run mode. In these situations, if you don't make the sale immediately, the emotion of the moment is gone as soon as you walk out the door. You won't have another opportunity to make the sale. Here's how Share of Heart can close one-shot sales:

▷ Pique your prospects' interest by learning about their needs.

▷ Sell them on how your product can enrich their lives.

▷ Excite them throughout the pitch by showing what the product has done for others.

▷ Reinforce the emotion of the pitch.

Successful infomercial producers are masters of emotion. Hard-sell inserts are placed into their "programs" three or four times at approximately six-minute intervals, usually at the commercial's most uplifting moments. They simply wear you down with their enthusiasm.

When you don't reinforce your product's benefits each of these four times, you open the door to your competition. This is true whether your product is a lightbulb, insurance, or advertising services. The principle of constant emotional reinforcement is the same. If you're a supplier and you don't return phone calls to reassure the buyer that you're constantly on the job, you're going to be out of business. One supplier of business services tells me he forces himself to call clients at least once a week. He may have nothing of great importance to say, but he knows his customers will lose faith in him if he doesn't say something—anything!

Selling to the heart does not make up for a badly designed product or one whose time has not come. In fact, it will hasten the demise of a poorly conceived product because the product will disappoint and never be bought again.

Share of Heart Comes Before the Product Is Built, Not After

The way you want your product to be perceived by consumers should be determined while the product is in the development stages—not later. Your emotional commitment to consumers is critical in every phase of the business, from product planning and development to marketing to research and development. It should be built into every marketing plan.

The positioning and core emotional benefits should be determined as a first step in marketing and product development. They should determine most aspects of the product. Your product should be engineered around your Share of Heart. Of course, many products that were built the opposite way—say, driven by engineering—have worked out. But almost every company has an extensive archive of products that looked truly exceptional on paper, but were ignored by consumers. These products became a solution searching for a problem. For instance, interactive TV, which was proclaimed the industry of the 1990s, has faded because of lack of consumer interest. People want to veg out in front of mindless TV shows, not talk back to them. People do, however, respond to the home selling networks like QVC and the Home Shopping Network. The pitchpeople have built a rapport with the home audience. Gimmicks like instant call-in testimonials emotionally involve the viewer at home. The home shopping networks are entertainment. Interactive TV takes thought—a chore best reserved for people who are using computers.

Share of Heart should be manifested in all parts of your product, from the packaging to the product itself. When you change the emotional hook in your product, you're actually creating a new product in the consumer's mind. This was proved by Coors Brewing Company—usually a savvy marketer. When draft-style canned beers became big, Coors changed its package design and the name of its flagship product to Coors Draft Style Beer. Bad move. Sales dropped. The consumer perception was that the product had changed.

How to Graph Share of Heart—Surprise, You Can't

So why, if Share of Heart is so important, do most companies ignore it? Because:

> ▷ You can't pull Share of Heart out of a quantitative research study (usually).
> ▷ It's hard to sell Share of Heart to management because it's difficult to back up with hard numbers.
> ▷ And they almost never teach about Share of Heart in business school because it can't be quantified.

Somewhere, somehow, it became common to think that emotion in selling is a nebulous, airy proposition that should be left to advertising agencies—after the product is created. That's wrong. Advertising agencies are in the business of selling media space and air time. They don't build products. What agencies won't admit is that the rationalization for a creative strategy often comes after the strategy is developed. It's like building a house around a nail. The standard procedure is to come up with three advertising campaigns: one that the agency likes, one that the clients will like, and one because three is a nice number. What about the consumer? Does the agency care? Can you, as a marketer, afford not to care?

Logic Versus Emotion

Consumers buy products for two reasons:

1. *The logical reason.* One product provides better benefits or services than another.
2. *The real reason.* The product provides emotional satisfaction.

That's why branded items are preferred, on average, ten times more than store brands. Arm & Hammer baking soda outsells all the other brands combined even though baking soda is a simple chemical. The brand conveys trust and authority. The generic brands seem almost naked and impersonal on their shelf next to the Arm & Hammer product. Perhaps we saw the Arm & Hammer product in our refrigerator so often that it made a permanent dent in our neural synapses. Ask consumers what they think about Johnson & Johnson products (Band-Aids, Baby Lotion, and others), and they'll tell you that Johnson & Johnson cares about you. It's a simple premise, but it's enormously powerful and profitable. That's why the company can offer line extension after line extension and know that the product will be tried.

Logic Is Not Enough

If you're looking for logic in the marketplace, you're on the wrong career path. Consumers follow their own convoluted logic. Actually, it's convoluted only to a marketer who doesn't understand what's going on in consumers' minds. The problem is, just when you think you've got it, you really don't. For example:

▷ Loading an orange juice with extra vitamins seems to be a sure thing—consumers are going to be drinking it anyway. But it's never been highly successful in the marketplace.

▷ The same people who eat Total, Müeslix, and Bran Flakes are also steady buyers of Froot Loops, Lucky Charms, and Cap'n Crunch.

▷ Consumers feel it's okay to eat rich desserts, but those same consumers will turn up their nose at most high-calorie drinks. That's why Mars flopped with Milky Way Milk Shakes.

▷ Consumers will give lip service to recycling and fighting pollution, but in the real world most won't pay extra for a recyclable container.

▷ If a product looks too good on the package, people will buy it, but represent the product faithfully on the package and nobody will buy it. In a weird way, people expect to be deceived. The movie is never as good as its trailer made it seem.

▷ If toothpaste or medicine tastes too good, people won't believe in it or let their kids use it. (This drove the people at Colgate crazy.)

▷ Rich taste in a cigarette or beer is good, but mention it in the context of food and it's considered unhealthy.

▷ Women will purchase a product positioned for men, e.g., razors, racquets, and menswear, but men will not purchase a product positioned for women.

Logic, Rationalizations, and Psychological Rewards

Buyers are neither consistent nor sensible in their purchase behavior. Not always, anyway.

Next door to my office are both a health club and a dessert bar. The bar has every pie, cake, pudding, and ice cream imaginable. The desserts are outrageously fatty and unhealthy. The dessert bar feeds off the health club. People spend an hour on exercise bikes (God knows why, you don't go anywhere) and head right to the dessert bar for coffee and whipped cream pies. Why? Because they feel that they earned the treat. Of course, if they didn't go to the dessert bar so often, they probably wouldn't have to torture themselves on the bike for so long.

They rationalize their indulgence by saying, "I just worked out for an hour. I deserve a treat."

Sure, all of America is on a diet. But a good percentage of these dieters buy Häagen Dazs. And the people who won't allow themselves the fatty ice cream can buy Häagen Dazs Sorbet. It may not be as rich as the regular ice cream, but the buyers enjoy the same kind of psychological rewards. When people want to treat themselves well, they often turn to the most prestigious, and usually priciest, brands in a category. Häagen Dazs meets this criterion. It is considered one of the most self-indulgent of frozen desserts. The foreign-sounding name contributes to the experience. By the way, the name Häagen Dazs is strictly a marketing ploy. Do you know what Häagen Dazs means? Nothing. Do you know why Häagen Dazs puts the two foreign-looking dots over the *a*? Because it looks foreign. And in what small Scandinavian town do elves zealously guard and make the Häagen Dazs flavors? The product is made in Woodbridge, New Jersey, and other sites in the United States and Canada.

It's human nature to want more than we have. That's why a low price can sometimes actually hurt sales. Consumers usually want the best they can buy. Notice I didn't say the best they can reasonably afford. Car salespeople usually show their prospective customers a higher-priced car than the buyer is looking for. The salesperson is hoping that the emotion that the car elicits will cause the customer to trade up to a better model than he or she originally wanted. The salesperson, of course, will help the customer rationalize the cost by talking about reliability and resale value.

Share of Heart can be a sensual tie-in, something you can see, feel, or hear. Or even smell. These can all be considered rewards. Yes, you can smell emotion. Part of the excitement of owning a new car is the new car smell. The smell comes from the evaporation of plasticizers in the vinyl dashboard, but no matter. The smell partially camouflages the fact that the buyer is going to be making obscene car payments for the next five years. And does anyone really buy a Mercedes for its "engineering"?

Perception Is Reality

The principle behind Share of Heart is simple. If consumers think something works better or tastes better, then it does work better or taste better. As this is being written, the hottest hair products are those that were originally created for horses. Yes, horses. It seems that 80 percent of the sales of Equine Shampoo, by Jheri Redding no less, is sold to women of the human persuasion. Bath & Body Works has a new Stables shampoo. The message is that if it's strong enough for horses and is made by a well-known company, it must be pretty good. Another hot consumer product is Udder Cream, sold by Wal-Mart, Walgreen's, and a host of other mass marketers. I don't even want to think what consumers are doing with it.

The consumer's perception of your product is everything, even when it's wrong. I was one of the creators of Lucky Dog dog food for Ralston-Purina. All dry dog foods from major companies are nutritionally just about equal. If you're a dog, they all taste about the same. (I'm guessing on that claim.) Our winning strategy was to develop a food with a variety of different shapes and textures. To be frank, when a dog slobbers over its food, it probably doesn't give a hoot that one shape is different from another or that the product has a rainbow of colors. Remember, dogs are color blind! But consumers care. Lucky Dog made the boring daily feeding routine a little more fun for the dogs' owners. The owners think that if they were dogs, this is what they would like. These people like to think they treat their dogs better than other dog owners do.

Supermarkets are now facing a marketing crisis brought on by this sort of consumer psychology. A large proportion of pet owners are buying their pet food at so-called pet food boutiques, like Petsmart. Because the salespeople wear badges, they are considered experts. Ralston has tried to fight back by creating a "serious" dog food called One that is sold in the dog food aisle of the standard supermarket. It's not selling well. People think, "If it's sold in a supermarket, how special can it be?" They would rather buy from a store-proclaimed "expert."

On the other end of the perception spectrum is the D.A.T. recording system. Back when compact discs became the standard of audio quality, the D.A.T. tape system was introduced. These were magnetic tapes, smaller than audiocassettes. They rivaled CDs in quality, but they failed to attract a large consumer audience. Because the medium was tape, consumers didn't feel that the D.A.T. system could deliver the same audio quality that they could get from the bright, shiny compact discs. Consumers were incorrect, but it didn't make a difference. Only a handful of sound engineers buy the product today.

Emotion: The Key to Impulse Sales

In an impulse product, the whole rationality of the purchase decision is short-circuited. The consumer has no time to think, only to react. You have to do everything you can to trigger that reaction. That's how L'Eggs pantyhose, with its cute plastic egg-shaped container, became the dominant force in the women's hosiery market. Share of Heart conquers the information overload we talk about by substituting images and feelings for words.

An impulse product must sell itself once—but *big-time*. You have to grab the browser with a searing emotional hook. Three of the contributors to the emotional hook are a strong name, the package, and positioning. They must get the product concept across and cut through the repetitive blather of other products on the shelf. The name should trigger an emotion with consumers. The package should act like a beacon on the shelf. Packaging is not the place to be subtle. The name and package should hit consumers like a brick.

If a product connects with consumers' lives at the key moment of decision, they're interested. Your positioning should call out the consumer's name and lifestyle, and your product sell should flow from this positioning. Say Godiva, and you instantly call up chocolate imagery. Godiva's glitzy foil and ribbons obscure the fact that it is an average-tasting confection. Say

Chivas Regal, and you are talking about a prestigious drink. The price, the packaging, and the advertising all add up to the image of a fine Scotch.

Having a new product that works better or does a new consumer trick is not enough anymore. You've got to feed the ego. Consumers need to feel good about themselves and fulfill their self-images. It's a basic human need.

Overintellectualizing your product features can be a deadly marketing flaw. Consumers are not buying features, they're buying benefits—but only as they perceive them. Adding a new gizmo to a product may send your engineering department into ecstasy, but it doesn't mean a thing if consumers can't find a reason for the feature—if they can't rationalize the extra expense.

Share of Heart in Low-Interest, Parity, and Commodity Products

Products like lightbulbs, toilet paper, and aspirin are often referred to as low-interest or low-involvement products. But in reality, there are no low-interest products, only boring writers and marketers. Parity products may actually be a safe way to marketing success, because there is already an established need. You don't have to test the waters. What you must do is give consumers a little something extra to differentiate your brand from the other brands. Toilet paper has been around awhile. Charmin gave it a little twist by making its paper softer than others.

Cole slaw and potato salad were considered commodity products, until the Orville Kent Company added a new Share of Heart to the category.

Supermarketing: From Salad to Salad Days

But, you may say, we are not selling branded goods. We are selling a commodity, like potato salad. A commodity can have a Share of Heart like a branded item when you offer consumers an emotional point of difference. That's what the Orville Kent family did. It was selling a deli salad product line to stores. You know the products: typical potato salad, cole slaw, etc. But Orville Kent came up with an inspiration: "Let's make our product sound better than the typical store product. We'll call ours Signature Salads . . . and we'll work with the store to make a more elegant presentation."

Competitors laughed. "Who cares? Potato salad is potato salad." But the retailers cared, and so did their customers. And it created a revolution at the deli counter. Orville Kent is now one of the biggest deli providers and has successfully branched out into other areas in which its store brands can be looked upon as just a little better than competitors'. The company can't keep up with the demand.

If you can add emotional panache to a low-priced category, you have a winner.

Consumers have to make a decision about every product they buy. For the brief ten seconds or so that they consider it, your product is the most important thing in their life. What could be of less interest than a toilet bowl cleaner? Yet Toilet Duck added personality to the category. S.C. Johnson has even created a drop-in-the-tank product shaped like (what else?) a duck.

We now have more tools available to us than ever to sell our product—packaging, research, promotion, technology. But we can learn about our customers only through the most advanced tool known—our minds. All it takes is well-placed questions and some stimuli, which we'll go over in detail in the next chapter.

Turning a Negative Into a Benefit

The word *negative* proclaims a value judgment. Somebody's negative can be someone else's positive. Natural foods is a huge industry created on a negative. Products aren't standardized. Prices are higher than for products grown and marketed to mass market stores. Fluid products like peanut butter separate in the jar. But there is a huge, targetable audience that wants only natural foods and is willing to pay a higher price. The hottest distribution outlets in the United States today are the giant health food emporiums. Prices are almost twice as high as at traditional supermarkets—even for the same items. People are patronizing these stores in droves because they believe that if the health food store carries the product, it must be something special. Perceptions belie reality—again.

Product negatives are a particular battlefront in the war between the marketing and research and development (R&D) divisions. Marketing wants R&D to create a perfect product. R&D says, sell what I can make. The proper way is to compromise and create a product that someone will buy. If you can't fix a product in manufacturing, you can often do it in the product's positioning.

For instance, an apparent consumer negative can be turned into a positive when we create a positive fantasy around it. Lightly flavored seltzers have been around since the 1960s. (This was what makers of no-calorie soda had left when the government made them remove cyclamates.) Smart marketers learned how to position their product as a clean, upscale, natural alternative to sugar-laden sodas. Same product, new perception. It was the alteration of consumer perceptions of what is refreshing that made it work. Caffeine, which was once considered a negative, is now being added to new soft drinks for an extra "kick."

While Share of Heart can't hide a product's tragic flaw, it can help you put a positive spin on your product's weaknesses. Larry's Italian fruit ices, sold in New York, have pits left by the manufacturing process. Larry points to them proudly: So fresh and fruity, it even has pits.

The Recipe for Success

Here's the recipe for a successful Share of Heart attack: 1/4 cup of reality, 3/4 cup of perception, then stir until blended. Most companies find a product, then identify the consumer perception and try to create a positioning around it. I say, find the consumer's hot button and perception of a product cate-

gory first. Then build a product or marketing program around that perception and hot button. Find a need first and then fill it.

If a positioning is effective, it can even generate a product. Plugra is a new kind of butter. It has a third more artery-hardening cholesterol than traditional butters. Yet the maker found a market in the people who can't get enough of the rich taste of butter. It defies all logical reason, but it works as a marketing opportunity because its marketers have tapped into an emotional vein.

Yes, Share of Heart is something special. It's marketing magic—especially to the bottom line.

Aware companies know that. That's why some brands have been around for almost a century. The good news is that smaller brands can overcome the power of the tried and true by using Share of Heart. AriZona (iced tea) and Mistic (juice beverage) achieved success in the face of intense competition from the megabrand soft drinks like Coke and Pepsi. Both AriZona and Mistic have created a counterculture image. It looks good and cool to carry around a bottle of either drink. They're fashion statements as much as cooling drinks. As of this writing, both companies are planning to go head-to-head against Coke and Pepsi in the carbonated beverage arena. It will be fun to see if either company can keep up the momentum and successfully compete.

A reverse Share of Heart scenario is happening with Snapple beverages. Snapple was created by a trio of marketers from Long Island. Since the three didn't have the financial clout of the big guns, they marketed mainly to mom-and-pop stores. Along the way, their beverage developed cachet among trendies. This sought-after cachet was encouraged with clever advertising and the constant introduction of new, offbeat flavors. Snapple's audience was never allowed to get bored. Then the business was peddled to Quaker. This corporate monolith was totally out of touch with Snapple's consumer base. Sales plummeted 15 percent almost immediately. Although Quaker continues to toss money into the Snapple venture, the brand will never be as powerful as it was two short years ago. New competition is continually eroding the loyalty of Snapple's customers.

Marketing Miscues: What Is Sara Lee?

Most of us grew up assaulted by the buttery taste of Sara Lee pound cake, chocolate cake, or cheesecake. Absolutely sinful. It was a world-class product. Yet something happened along the way. The company hired a series of managers who cared little about the brand name. They milked the brand with any line extension they could think of.

A funny thing happened after that: Sara Lee lost its brand equity. Ask a consumer what Sara Lee stands for and you'll get blank stares. The Sara Lee people continue to launch one dud after another and wonder why they can't get a foothold in any particular category. It's not that the new Sara Lee products are bad. For a company *not* named Sara Lee, they are acceptable. It's that the new products they've come up with don't stand for anything. They have no emotional link to the mother brand. The Pavlovian response, "This is going to be good because it's made by Sara Lee," is gone.

If you want to keep your emotional involvement with consumers, you have to develop a product that won't lead consumers to say, "Why did they come out with this?" They should say, "That's what I expect from Sara Lee." Is Sara Lee special to today's consumers? Nah. It's just another company in the store. You don't go to McDonald's for steak au poivre. You don't patronize the Sara Lee brand for a dry piece of fat-free snack cake.

Putting the Pieces Together to Create a Blockbuster

I was in an immensely crowded restaurant the other day. It looked so easy: Serve decent food with a pleasant atmosphere and people will come rushing to your door. But in the real world, it doesn't work like that. Before the restaurant opened, the owner had to decide who her target market was, what kind of food she had to prepare, and what to charge. She had to make key decisions about such matters as decor and even the appropriate bathroom fixtures.

Even then, the restaurateur was not finished. She had to keep tabs on her customers to make sure they were satisfied. If they weren't, they would never be back.

It was the totality of the dining experience that would create repeat customers. It is the totality of the buying experience that will keep your customers coming back for more.

That is your Share of Heart.

Yes, Share of Heart is something special. It's marketing magic—especially to the bottom line.

▷ 2

Fifteen Hot Buttons
to Push

American Indians have used objects called fetishes for more than a thousand years to help reshape their inner selves. A fetish is a hand-carved depiction of an animal. It is a symbolic carrier of a message. Indians would carve the symbol of the animal whose attributes they aspired to possess. The badger is aggressive and industrious. The eagle represents a soaring spirit. The mountain lion symbolizes resourcefulness and leadership.

The power and strength of a fetish is obtained by placing the nostrils of the fetish to one's mouth and taking deep breaths.

We rarely use fetishes anymore. Instead, we use brands and products as symbols for the qualities we wish to attain. Now it's Corvettes instead of mountain lions.

Images and emotions are your source of power in the marketing world. Create a strategic product model by learning what your customers want and fulfilling those desires. This is your emotional prototype. The emotional prototype should be written down and used as a guide for marketing and R&D. It should be created before you spend money on the whole product or marketing program.

Our wants are great motivators. It may take a little digging, but if you discover what customers want, then you can work hard to provide it. A human being is a wanting animal. As soon as one need is satisfied, another one comes to take its place. This process is unending. It continues from birth to death.

When you learn what motivates your market, you can create the images or pictures you need to send to make buyers want your product. You'll usually want to find logical reasons behind the motivations. It's not always possible. In fact, these motivations may go against your best marketing instincts. Don't worry about it. You don't need to personally agree with the message to make it effective.

Stay an arm's length from your product. In marketing, managers tend to get too close to the products they manage or sell. The product and positioning come to seem too simple. They then try to overcomplicate the product or strategy by looking past the simple solution. They provide long-winded rationalizations for *physical* product benefits because they believe consumers want them. You know what? They don't. Marketers are afraid that consumers will look past the blatant emotional sell. They won't. That the product works for them is enough reinforcement for consumers.

A product should be treated as a superhero. Speak to the qualities your customers aspire to as if your product already has them. You can solve a situation by identifying it and symbolizing it (like the Indians with their fetishes) far better than you can with a lot of copy emphasizing features.

This chapter is *not* about basic survival needs like food, shelter, and water. It's because these needs have been met quite well in most countries that we have to shoot for emotional bull's-eyes. Many times we put our emotional needs even before our health requirements, e.g., by smoking, heavy drinking, overeating.

There are a great many psychological needs that people aspire to fulfill—far too many to list in one chapter. But the following turn-ons have worked time and time again. They've created opportunities for a great many marketers.

The only consumer interest is self-interest. You'll find that some of these hot buttons overlap. Despite the marketer's penchant for categorizing things, marketing in the real world is not always cut-and-dried.

The Fifteen Hot Buttons

Hot Button 1: The Desire for Control

Many people think their lives are out of control. They don't know where they're going or how they're going to get there. This is not good. Feelings of loss of control are synonymous with a fear of the unknown. People equate loss of control with loss of power over their own destiny or the destiny of their loved ones.

Cellular phones are one of the hottest products today. Of course, many are sold to businesspeople whose egos are so overdeveloped that they believe they can't be disconnected from their businesses for more than a minute or so.

But the growth of the product is not being driven as much by business sales as by the ordinary consumer. A cellular phone offers unparalleled access to control by users: control over their families, control for their family. For example, when I bought my cellular phone (OK, I'm the egotistical type), my daughter wanted one. "All right," I said, "give me a reason." She said, "When I'm driving home from college, I may have a breakdown on a dark highway." This was a superb rationalization. She got the phone the next day.

Further research into the cellular phone business shows that control over difficult situations is the driving force behind sales. Buyers often are paranoid about their vulnerability to bad situations (e.g., strange men waiting on one's doorstep). With a mobile phone, the scared consumer can call the police or a nearby friend. The cellular phone user feels that he or she will never be totally isolated in a precarious situation. In an auto accident, people can call the police, a hospital, or a friend to help deal with sometimes irate and irrational drivers. By offering basic rates (about $19.95 per month), cellular phone providers have fulfilled this basic need for control and safety.

The control issue is also driving the home business industry, which has grown by leaps and bounds. People no longer think of "company as provider." They want to be their own provider. They are learning that they have to look out for themselves and their own interests because corporate America won't look out for them. They are purchasing mini-offices in the home and scaled-down office equipment for personal use in hopes of starting a business and creating an income that is not at the mercy of irate bosses and corporate layoffs.

Airplane pilots give out information on what's delaying things and where you are in the sky to make you feel you have control even when you are 30,000 feet above the ground.

Even a carpet cleaner can help solve a control dilemma. While the person who cleans the house can't stop dogs from doing things on rugs that they're not supposed to do, he or she can practice damage control by using a rug protectant or a cleaner positioned for "dogs, cats, and rambunctious kids." The ultimate control in dealing with a cat's bodily functions is a new electronic device that automatically cleans litter and seals cat droppings in a plastic bag.

Hot Button 2: Revaluing

In the early 1950s, they toddled. In the 1960s, they marched. During the 1970s and 1980s, they built careers and families. Now, the baby boomers are entering yet another phase in their lives: revaluing.

Baby boomers are approaching fifty, and they're taking stock of their lives. Finally they're saying, "I have a chance to be happy." They are beginning to think that looking to past comforts and happiness may help them find happiness in the present. They're returning to products and entertainment that offer them contentment and familiarity. It's part of an overall revaluing of their lives.

This revaluing by boomers is creating boom markets for familiar products.

The trend is largely responsible for the growing success of Nick at Nite on Nickelodeon, with comfort programming like *The Mary Tyler Moore Show*, *The Dick Van Dyke Show*, and *Bewitched*.

This "revaluing" hot button will drive behavior and purchasing decisions in this country for the remainder of this decade and into the next century.

Baby boomers will gravitate toward products that are familiar (and therefore comforting), but often with a contemporary twist, like sodas with a more sophisticated appeal. But they will still harken back to older favorites like Cheerios, Cap'n Crunch, and Froot Loops or older flavors with a new twist, like Frosted Cheerios or Cinnamon Life.

These people also want greater control over their lives. They have learned that they have to look out for themselves and focus on what's important in their lives—family, financial security, and health.

Homes are being downsized in favor of smaller, equally expensive properties filled with creature comforts like elaborate multimedia centers. Baby boomers striving for a more simple life will continue their exodus from urban locations to the Southwest, Florida, and Montana as a way of simplifying and improving the quality of their lives.

As baby boomers age and their children leave the nest, the divorce rate will soar because "revaluing" baby boomers will put their personal happiness first and choose to end difficult marriages.

Yet baby boomers are the lost generation as a marketing target. Even Pepsi admits that it has no plans to target this highly affluent market. That's because most of Pepsi's marketers are not part of the baby boomer generation.

As baby boomers continue to revalue their lives, emotional connections to purchases should drive manufacturers to develop products and strategies that enhance the consumer's perception of a better lifestyle, such as educational toys for grandchildren and healthier foods. The trend towards neutraceuticals (nutrient-based food products) is driven by the motive of preventive maintenance for old bodies.

Hot Button 3: The Excitement of Discovery

They say a true intellectual is one who can listen to the *William Tell* Overture without thinking of the Lone Ranger. My idea of a gourmet is one who can dig into a Cracker Jack box without first checking out the prize inside. The joy of discovery is uncovering the unexpected and finding a source of physical and emotional power.

The new product business is totally based on discovery. This is why new products are so exciting to consumers. Words like *introducing, at last,* and *new* in ads are far more than bromides. They bring increased attention to almost any new product or positioning.

The joy of discovery means that almost any new product or service will generate at least passing interest. The chance of discovering something unique is why consumers prowl supermarket aisles instead of just grabbing the one product they came into the store for.

It's relatively easy to enhance your product when you factor in "discover" points. It can be as simple as giving your product a new benefit the other guy hasn't thought of yet or adding an extra unit of a product. Cereal manufacturers now offer prize collections in their boxes rather than simple premiums. The buyer never knows exactly what she or he will discover.

When a consumer unearths something, it also generates strong word of mouth. When a person talks about something he or she discovers, that person gets to feel important for exposing this new find. Avon's Skin So Soft was found to be effective at repelling bugs (it's also a decent paint remover). The message traveled quickly from customer to customer. Sales spread faster than they would have if Avon had released a new bug repellent. Some time ago, WD-40 was discovered to be an effective arthritis pain reliever as well as a household lubricant. While WD-40 would never admit it or publicize the fact, it gave the brand a new selling appeal.

A discovery is also a new way to beat the system. Kerosene heaters were a big item a few years ago. People discovered the enormous heat output they generated and rushed out to buy the product. They loved not having to pay the oil, gas, or electric company.

Hot Button 4: I'm Better Than You

You are what you buy. That's a primary tenet of marketing to the heart. Overwhelmingly, the means of choice for gaining status is consumer goods. People are willing to pay dearly to enhance themselves in the eyes of their peers.

Prestige or status sales cut through all income levels. Whether your customers are considered upscale or downscale is no barrier to making a product appeal through prestige. It's all relative. In some socioeconomic groups, large flashy gold jewelry is considered a status symbol. In other groups, small antique (valuable, yet understated) gemstones may be de rigueur.

The Optima card was supposed to be a Visa card with an attitude—the first rolling balance charge card from American Express—a charge card that gave users revolving credit. But consumers felt that it was nothing special—just about anyone with any kind of American Express card could get one. It wasn't even as classy as a Visa Gold.

American Express lost an immeasurable amount of prestige when it introduced the Optima card. It ran diagnostic interactive consumer groups to learn how to make the Optima card more helpful to various cardmembers. The respondents were Green Cardmembers (the basic membership), Gold Cardmembers (the advanced membership), and Platinum Cardmembers (the super-advanced membership—you have to own a small country). The Platinum Cardmembers actually sat separately from Green Cardmembers.

Whether you approve or not, status seeking is a dynamic part of our lives. Products are worn like ties—to be displayed and to exert power. Most people have a basic human need to stand out from the crowd.

Create products and positionings that put consumers on a pedestal for trying your product. Liquor companies have long known that. Vodka, for example, is, by definition, neutral and tasteless. Yet consumers, especially in low-income areas, will go for the name brand.

The move toward generic brands continues to die a slow, lingering death as supermarkets' marketing techniques become more sophisticated. Supermarkets are creating their own brands—super store brands. They've learned that a positive, upscale brand perception can be more appealing than a low price. Loblaw's, in Canada, has developed a unique private-label program that offers a premium version of products to enhance the supermarket's store brands and their image.

In a marketing strategy based on status, it's important to reinforce the product benefits and let consumers rationalize the extra cost. People buy Mercedes cars because they think such a car gives them prestige, and they justify the expense by talking about engineering. Membership in a prestigious country club can be rationalized by saying that it may lead to new business contacts.

Hot Button 5: Family Values

This political hot button is also a driving consumer force. The continuity of family relationships is one of the strongest consumer motivations. But today's vision of family togetherness is based more on media treatment of the fantasy of family life than on any reality. Reruns of *Leave It to Beaver* and *The Brady Bunch* define our ideal of family life. Beaver's and Wally's big crises came when Wally couldn't get a prom date or when Beaver tried to hide a newly found frog from his mom.

But there is trouble in familyland. The family breakfast is dead, and the family dinner is soon to be a casualty. While 40 percent of Americans families share dinner at the end of the day at least once a week, the economics of the two-paycheck family means that at least one of the dinner providers is going to be too tired to do much cooking or socializing.

Family problems encompass more serious matters than what to do with a frog. According to *Why They Buy*, by Robert Settle and Pamela Albeck, only one in twenty families fits the stereotype of a single-marriage, two-parent, two-child household.

But as usual, you must market to the dream—consumers want to close their eyes to the reality. The dream is the nuclear family sharing family dinners, not vying for time in front of the TV or the computer. Actually a case can be made that the media that have so implanted false family values in the minds of Americans have helped keep us together. In the 1950s and 1960s, families had only one TV and were forced to watch it together (a new definition of quality time).

Quality time with families is still of utmost importance to Americans, even if the family is more myth than actuality. Marketing to this myth is what has made Disney so successful and has given rise to the Sunday family brunch at the local Shoney's.

The New York Times commented on the widespread trend of taking more than the kids on the family cross-country drive vacation. Increasingly, cars carry three generations of family members—which probably leads to an increased number of bathroom stops. People (but not the older baby boomers) are making a great effort to spend quality time together as a family.

Consumers are trying to re-create the image of family values though artificial means—for example, by reproducing the types of food they remember from childhood. But the meals they remember are not mom's twelve-hour homemade chicken soup or grandma's homemade pasta sauces. Memories of childhood meals are attached to processed foods, not the made-from-scratch dinners of a generation before. That means you can sell the pleasure of a processed food as bringing the family together. The processed nature of these products might actually increase their appeal to some shoppers.

A Gallup poll asked: "If you were offered a slice of pie to share with anyone in the world . . . who would you choose?" The answer most given was—surprise—my husband/wife.

In a recent study on developing and positioning a new fireplace insert, it was the vision of the family sitting in front of the hearth that turned most consumers on.

The family unit is far from dead. It is evolving. Marketers must sell a vision of the family, not as it is, but as consumers wish it would be.

Hot Button 6: *Need for Belonging*

When James Taylor wrote "You've Got a Friend," an anthem of a sort in the 1970s, he didn't know he was writing a marketing essay.

Many people play team sports for the camaraderie of the sport and the desire to belong. Recently several groups of adult consumers were asked if they would rather be on a winning team of gung ho personalities who went their separate ways after the game, or a losing team that got together after the game for good times. Most of the people chose the latter.

Americans are the joiningest people in the world. Proof is probably in your wallet. How many clubs do you belong to? How many associations? Do you have a Gold Card or a Platinum Card?

We want to be among people who are like ourselves. Developing an affinity group is an effective way to market your product. If you have a group, you have a targetable audience.

The enormously successful computer bulletin board America Online calls itself a community. Over 6 million people make up this community; they have started many subgroups where they communicate with people who share the same interests.

The strongest affinity is age. At a party or an event, people will gravitate toward other people of the same age. That's why all the people in all of your communications work should be screened for the right age profile.

The desire to belong is also the reason for the upsurge in licensed athletic wear. People are showing their loyalty and affinity to the people wearing the same gear and declaring the same loyalties.

Hot Button 7: Fun, Novelty, Stimulation

Among the toughest appeals to sell to management is the desire to have fun with a product. Marketing is serious business. Who has dollars to waste on frivolity? Yo, lighten up. Don't take yourself and your product so seriously. As you saw with Toilet Duck, you can have fun with your product *and* make money. Almost any product can be fun if we get back to the child within us and appeal to the child in the consumer.

The whole reason for adding fun to a product is to enhance the buyer's perception of pleasure and satisfy her or his need to be stimulated. That's the marketing explanation. The real explanation is that fun is . . . well, fun. Consumers need a break from everyday life's routine. If your product can provide a few moments of pleasure, this can make it stand out from the others.

This can be as simple as adding a scent (provided you've found a rationalization), a new taste, a new texture. The more senses you can get involved in a product, the more emotionally involved a consumer gets. Even something as deadly dull as riding an exercise bike can be fun when you add a computer-generated race game to the handlebars. (Nah, it's still a pain.)

With all the bad news on the front pages, most newspaper readers turn to either the sports section (the adult toy store), the comics, or the crossword puzzle. The desire to have fun is its own motivation.

Fun can be in the alchemy your product provides. Who doesn't like the addition of magic to life? Products that change color, a tablet that magically effervesces—even a toilet bowl that

turns blue. These all add fun to the product and can add up to hefty sales.

Fun can also be manifested in the name of the product. The name Gobblestix, a turkey product targeted to kids and moms, may be simplistic to us marketing mavens—but not to moms and kids.

Fun is important in business-to-business scenarios too. Companies often choose a supplier because he or she seems like "one of us"—you can have a good time with this person after work. Why does this matter? Having a good time with a supplier helps businesspeople bond together. It helps build relationships.

J. Barry Golliday is senior vice president of Information Resources, one of the largest compilers of consumer purchasing data. He makes many presentations to marketers. He says one of the biggest issues in brand management is how marketers can have fun at their job—it's an even bigger issue than how they can be successful. That means you can add fun to business-to-business products and presentations. An accountant friend—a right-brained sort—just bought a multicolored keyboard for his computer. It looks like it was made by Barney the Dinosaur. But to the accountant, it adds a bit of novelty to the workday and thus is worth the money.

When you add fun or amusement to your product, you have a better chance of bonding with your customer. That results in increased business.

Hot Button 8: Time

Time is of the essence. So is organization. You can't create time. But you can sure lose it.

What most marketers see as convenience products are actually time management tools. Poverty of time is a huge handicap in the 1990s. Saving time is one of the biggest motivators of men and women, ages twenty-five to forty-five. This is particularly true for women in their childbearing years. Taking care of the kids and putting dinner on the table is still considered the woman's job. It doesn't matter if the woman works forty hours a week, attends PTA meetings in the evening, and is writing computer software in her spare time. Even prominent women executives in so-called liberated homes are trying to play super-mom. These women, despite their business standing, consider parenting their prime job and proof of their importance and worth.

For men, freeing hours means more quality time with the kids or being able to work harder and longer and make more money.

But saving someone time means more than just putting cheese in an aerosol can. Your product has to perform as well as—or even better than—products that don't save the customer hours of preparation. Tom Bush and Mark Schweiger created a product called Ready Crisp Fully Cooked Bacon for the microwave. These were bacon strips that cooked up in a microwave in about five seconds. In the 1980s, several companies had failed with this concept. One obstacle all encountered was that the package is lighter than most uncooked bacon packages. It gave the false impression (remember, perception is everything) that consumers were not getting their money's worth. Schweiger and Bush solved the problem by putting tempting product photos and a large "20 slices" descriptor on the package. For reassurance, they put a clear window on the back, so that people could see the quality of their product.

If your product can save someone time and deliver quality the way our bacon makers did, you can have a hit on your hands. The paucity of time has created a major market for books on tape. People can listen in the car and turn downtime into useful time.

Closely related to saving time is the organization motivation. For some reason, people have a perverse need to sort, categorize, and stow. It makes them feel that they're in control of their lives (check out hot button 1 again). If you have a product that organizes, the most effective way to show the benefit is with a simple, dramatic, before-and-after product shot on all of your sales material—and on the package itself.

The Day Runner and Filofax people have built their businesses on time saving, organization, and control. Whether these organizers actually make a person more productive, I can't say. But businesspeople love to show off their fully scheduled Day Runner to show how busy they are—status seeking again. (Hot button 4—notice how motivations tie together nicely?)

Hot Button 9: The Desire to Get the Best That Can Be Got

There is a certain mystique about buying the best one can reasonably afford. It's different from the desire for status because it involves owning a treasure strictly for the personal satisfaction of owning the best. In every category there is an "est" factor. It is the brightest, fanciest, fastest product in a given category—the quintessential. Buying the best is a tool of one-upmanship. You can't be one-upped if you have the finest. As a marketer, you must provide cues that demonstrate why your product is the finest in its category.

When Sony invented the compact disc, it revolutionized the recording industry. The disk is bright and shiny. Now record companies are further enhancing the CD by offering gold-plated special editions—for the people who want the best, naturally.

The Harley-Davidson is the quintessential motorcycle, even if, as a Harley engineer said in *Business Week*, "the new Japanese knock-offs are as good as, if not better than, Harleys." Japanese motorcycle makers know what they're up against. Said Robert Moffitt, vice president of sales for Kawasaki Motors, USA, "The Harley audience buys on emotional and lifestyle issues." Harley-Davidson even has patents on the distinctive sound of its engines.

The older people get, the more willing they become to splurge on things that they denied themselves while the kids were at home. A brand new owner of a Harley, a woman of about sixty, gave the reason behind her purchase simply and cogently. "I got me a Harley. Now I'm classy."

Hot Button 10: The Desire to Be the Best (You Can Be)

There was a headline in a recent issue of *Inc.* that was exceptional. It was "Picture Yourself a Success." It was the personification of the rewards of self-achievement.

Self-achievement is a major goal for most people. "Be the best you can be" is more than a slogan—it's a statement that many people take seriously.

The saying goes, "It's not whether you win or lose, it's how you play the game." Not so. It's whether you win or lose. The real phrase should be, "It's not whether you win or lose, it's whether I win."

There's a reason teachers gave us gold stars and ratty paper certificates when we did a task well. It made us feel that we had accomplished something. Business psychologists know that we seek praise from our bosses as much as we want a good paycheck.

Intrinsic rewards, such as a compliment from a boss or a coach, spouse, or mother, are far more likely to motivate people for the long term than extrinsic rewards, such as money. That's why many people hesitate to retire, even though the bills have been taken care of. They need the intrinsic rewards of working and applying themselves to a task.

In the popular TV-series-cum-movie-series-cum-more-TV-series, *Star Trek*, there was an implied message: Man has the ability to explore new areas and do things in a way in which they have not been done before. It's a message about self-achievement. It's a strong message.

A whole slew of products can be positioned as offering to make users the best they can be, whether it's on the job, on the sports field, or at home. A cake mix that offers a new texture or flavor, a new kind of craft or hobby, or a new software program that promises to enhance a job all offer ways of making the buyer the best he or she can be.

A subset of this is the desire to break a bad habit. A bad habit can be sloth, poor eating habits, smoking, or a myriad of other things. (Actually, a bad habit is anything your partner does that you don't like.) Bad habits are considered character imperfections. Diet plans and smoking cessation programs are still proliferating as more people try to rid themselves of bad habits. In fact, 90 percent of all diet programs fail. But the desire to break a bad habit and improve ourselves in some way is a goal most of us aspire to. A consumer who gets the results he or she wants gets a special satisfaction: "Gee, all that work paid off."

Hot Button 11: Love of Cosmo and All That It Stands For

According to *The New York Times*, even blue-green algae do it. Do what? Bond with each other to have baby algae. According to the article, blue-green algae have to get together in order to reproduce. Of course, we all know that blue-green algae are asexual and reproduce by cloning themselves. When they want to do this, they gather together as a group—sort of a one-celled singles bar.

We may have come a long way toward sexual equality, but you'd never know it by reading some of the articles at the supermarket checkout counter. (Speed reading really pays off when you're on line to pay for a quart of milk.) Men's magazines talk about getting women, and women's magazines talk about getting men. They all talk about how much weight Oprah is losing.

In the magazines, sex and love are strongly correlated. These magazines must have their pulse on how to attract their readers because sales at the checkout counter are impulse sales.

While it is not politically correct to say it, sex still sells and will always sell.

Hot Button 12: The Nurturing Response

What do the following have in common: Lucky Dog dog food, Band-Aids, and a bowl of hot, steaming cereal? They all have to do with nurturing. The nurturing instinct is one of the great pulls of life. The desire to give care is strong, probably even stronger than the urge to get care.

Who does not feel guilty when he or she passes over the numerous ads for charities to feed hungry children? (Look at the ads—big eyes again.)

How you tie in the nurturing aspect of your product depends on the age and sex of your target group. For instance, single women in their thirties are concerned about their biological clocks. Many products should be tied into the joy of having children.

The 1990s man in his thirties is also a target for a nurturing approach. According to *The New York Times*, 90 percent (most of these probably passed out) of married men witness the birth of their babies, and 80 percent of men want to have a better relationship with their children than they had with their own dads. In the 1990s, men are supposed to be enhancing their feminine side, whatever that means. To be politically correct is to embrace one's sensitive side.

Products to be considered under the needs for nurturing are:

▷ Those that give care—products like TheraFlu and Vicks.
▷ Those than can provide comfort—foods like potatoes and pasta.
▷ Those that provide growth to any living thing. Miracle-Gro plant food is, in a way, a nurturing product.

Even a mundane fabric softener can be tied to nurturing. Lever Brothers created the name Snuggle for its fabric softener and gave it a nurturing appeal. Lever then devised its teddy bear symbol to continue to play right into our hearts.

The baby boomers, a growth market, are a prime target for products of a nurturing type, since many of them are or soon will be grandparents. They are prime targets for a "grandma purchase." A grandma purchase is a product that is too expensive, or even too esoteric, for the parents of a child to buy themselves. It can be an expensive toy, a book, or even a video game. Toymakers have learned to tie the sell into a learning experience, which is part of nurturing because it's the nourishment of the mind.

Travel can be viewed as a nurturing experience. Club Med started out as a single swingers' haven. These singles eventually married and had children. (Cause and effect of Club Med?) Club Med now positions some of its clubs as places for families to come together. These clubs feature crafts, movies, and the opportunity to learn a foreign language. This is travel as a learning experience for the entire family.

PPP is a company run by Judi Cohen. She markets many products under the nurturing banner. She has developed little stickers as toilet training aids. The child gets the sticker when he uses the toilet correctly. (M&M's have often been used as bribes to foster potty training.) One of the ways she marketed the product was to give out coupons for the product to toilet manufacturers. Sales proved excellent. She has since expanded into behavior modification products that allow parents to gently correct a child's inappropriate behavior and is working with Wal-Mart to develop a parenting section in its stores.

Even a product as mundane as shoelaces can be marketed as a nurturing product. Ms. Cohen also markets elastic shoelaces, which she bills as being so easy, children don't get frustrated tying their own shoes.

Hot Button 13: A Chance to Start Over With a Clean Slate

A person who has no regrets is a person who has not yet left the womb. Consumers and business buyers carry a great deal of physical and emotional baggage with them. A product can help a person start over, or it can be a symbol of starting over.

The credit card people and the mortgage people are playing the start-over card with extreme success. Many banks are offering secured cards that allow people with a negative credit history to have the same convenience as those with traditional credit cards. But the sell doesn't stop there. The people who obtain these cards feel that they are also rebuilding their past credit history—getting a second chance.

But getting a chance to start over is not limited to financial products. Weight-reducing clubs and nutrition products all promote the feeling of "discovering a new you." Cars can be promoted as being symbolic of starting a new way of life.

Cosmetic companies have long embraced the desire to start over. Each day offers people a chance to reinvent themselves with a new look or a chance to remove wrinkles and blemishes for a "new you."

Ads for home business products can stress the need to start over by working for oneself. Our whole financial system does this too; bankruptcy gives both businesspeople and consumers a way of rebirth. By the way, this book ends with a Chapter 11 (the most common kind of business bankruptcy). I'm not sure if I like the way that sounds.

Hot Button 14: Reason and Intelligence

This whole book is about emotion and the irrationality of the human purchase decision, and now we're talking about appeals to the intellect? Yes. Because people want to think they're smart.

Knowledge comes in many forms. While educating consumers is expensive, it can be done in ads, on the package, and even in hangtags. A case in point is the American Pork Council. Prior to the introduction of its slogan, "The Other White Meat," pork sales were hitting the skids. Consumers equated pork with fatty bacon and greasy spareribs. The Pork Council then set out to educate consumers. It repositioned pork as a light meat with a great deal of protein. Sales went (I can't resist) hog-wild. Consumers were proud of themselves for learning something new.

Frank Perdue also did a marvelous job of educating consumers. He created a frenzy in a commodity-style category by convincing consumers that the natural color of a chicken should be yellow. When consumers placed a Perdue yellow chicken next to the whitish chicken from a competitor, the other chicken paled by comparison. The Perdue buyer knew that he or she was buying the best. (By the way, Perdue chickens are yellow because they are fed crushed marigold petals.)

According to a U.S. News/CNN Gallup poll, 67 percent of American adults visited a public library at least once in the past year. Motivating most of these visitors is a desire to learn more than they currently know—the knowledge to get more out of life than they are already receiving by educating themselves about some aspect of their lives.

Hot Button 15: Self-Nurturance and the Ability to Stay Ageless and Immortal

This is perhaps our oldest motivation. It becomes more effective, naturally, as people age. Older people are more willing to spend money on things that make them feel good about themselves. They have been raising families and working hard for so long; now they are ready to say, "Hey, how about me?"

Products and positionings that offer physical, mental, or biological paths to making aging easier will always be effective.

When you market to older people (an older person is anyone older than me), the trick is to avoid at any cost making them feel old. Every generation resists aging, but the baby boomers are going to rage against it. Playing the youth angle too hard also misses the mark. It's not so much about being young as it is about a desire to maintain a certain lifestyle. People are getting older, but they don't want to change the way they live because of it. An example of a marketing campaign that plays to this "I won't age" mentality is a Tylenol commercial depicting a fortysomething man jogging after knee surgery. That's what mature people are like: finding themselves getting older but trying not to let their age slow them down.

In an episode of the classic TV show *The Twilight Zone*, an aged man was given the opportunity to get a new, more useful body. He turned it down because his equally old wife could not get one. He might have wanted to get younger, but he didn't want to leave his past life totally behind.

Give the Power to Fly

This chapter was about marketing successfully by giving consumers the power to fly. This can mean the ability to upgrade one's lifestyle for greater rewards. It can mean the ability to do one's job better. It can mean the ability to get just a little more out of life.

There are a great many emotional needs you can satisfy when you look beyond the basics of your product. People build their lives around consumer products and sometimes use them to reinforce their entire emotional foundation.

You can build a business when you offer your customers the chance to fly with your product by learning and pushing the right emotional hot buttons.

Straight-to-the-Heart Marketing Research

The soldier stood at the airport gate. He was going to meet his soul mate. Although they had never met, he and Abigail had corresponded for over a year, exchanging their deepest thoughts and feelings.

He had never heard her voice or seen her picture. She had steadfastly refused to send a picture, saying in her letters, "If you love me, my looks won't matter. If I am beautiful, I'd always fear that you loved me only for my looks. That kind of love I do not want. If I'm homely and you rejected me, I would feel that you corresponded with me only as an amusement for your lonely days."

They were to meet at noon today. She was to wear a red rose on her coat.

When the plane pulled in, the first woman out was a woman of classic beauty, with golden tresses. She was resplendent, beautifully dressed in a green coat and suit. She turned to the soldier. "Going my way, soldier?" she asked. He wanted to.

But then a matronly woman, about fifty—much older than he—followed her. Plump and grey, she wore a rose on a dowdy, moth-eaten coat.

He was torn. Which woman would he go to?

"I'm Lieutenant Smith, Abigail," he said to the woman wearing the rose.

The woman smiled. "I'm sorry, young man. I don't know what you're talking about. The girl in green asked me to wear this rose." She pointed to the beautiful young woman. "She said it was some kind of test."

This chapter is also about testing. Like Abigail's test, it is about uncovering the secrets of the consumer's heart. A successful marketing effort begins with keen probing into the hearts of your customers or prospective customers. It climaxes with fulfilling a need. This will become your preemptive market benefit.

The Trouble With Research

Corporate researchers have a great many high-tech tools at their disposal. These are about as accurate in determining the future as if you called the Psychic Friends' Network. As one manager told me, "Most research is like looking through a rear-view mirror." You know where you've been, but you don't know what's around the bend. Modern research techniques are quite ineffective at dealing with the hearts of consumers. They generate a great number of reports (and acetate decks for overhead projectors), but generating these reports is the sole purpose of much research. Few of the reports are actually read, except by fellow researchers or brand managers who search with magnifying glasses for the one sentence in the report that supports their preconceived idea.

Even so-called perceptual mapping, while it looks good on paper, is not effective at getting into the hearts of specific consumer segments. Perceptual mapping is a way of graphing consumer emotions about your product. It's much too abstract to connect with the real world of marketing. All the modeling and mapping in the world is not going to do you any good if you can't generate key insights into your customers' buying psyche and connect them with your product.

Time also lessens the value of research. Most research is outdated six months after a report is finally produced. The changing marketplace sees to that. Consumers are fickle. They may love you one day and ignore you the next. A project can take six months or more, and a report can take three to six months to prepare. After the research project is completed a month then goes by before a manager gets around to reading it; we can be talking about a lag time of as much as a year. That's a long time to basically ignore your customers. In that time there will be new products solving customer needs that hadn't even been thought of when the research was started. That means you have to start the entire research cycle again—to produce yet more outdated findings.

Changing attitudes means you have to carry out constant dialogs with your target consumers. This is something your competitors know. (Or maybe your competitors don't know it, but can you take that chance?)

But what's worse than using weak or outdated research is doing no research at all and relying on "common knowledge" about your customers and their needs. This happens quite often with novice entrepreneurs. They spend their life savings developing a product for which there is no need. Surprisingly, previously successful managers also fall into the "I know all about my customers" trap. They're so heady after their first success, they think they can do it again by the seat of their pants. Few entrepreneurs capture this lightning in the bottle a second time. (One entrepreneur who has succeeded in several business ventures is Gino Paolucci, who founded Chun King, Jeno's Pizza Rolls, and Michelina's. He's just launched another Chinese food venture called Yu Sing.)

You may be thinking that I'm a bit negative here, but in the past twenty years, with all of the alleged research innovations at the businessperson's disposal, the 90 percent new product failure rate has remained unchanged. Something is wrong here.

Stimulate and You Shall Find

Effective to-the-heart research does not have to be much more sophisticated than Abigail's simple and informal method in the opening story of this chapter. A cardinal mistake that many marketers make is to field a questionnaire survey in the faint hope of determining the reasons consumers make the choices they do. Buyers' genuine motives are not usually uncovered by direct questioning because consumers usually aren't aware of the real reasons they purchase something. Many consumers don't know that they on emotion or would never admit to it. This doesn't prevent you from measuring consumer motivation. It just means that you have to pry the information out of them by showing them various kinds of real-world stimuli.

The stimuli—also called probes because they help you probe into the consumer's heart and head—should consist of real-world "faux" ads (or other reaction devices) (see Figure 3-1), couched in a language your target market understands.

The reason behind using these stimuli is simple: They get consumers to react to your product and your product's message rather than intellectualize about what they *think* are their buying motives. Most of the brain deals with perception—the input of material we sense and organize. This perception remains latent until we stimulate the brain to make the perceptions come to the surface. The stimulus becomes a link, or trigger, to the person's heart.

For instance, you can ask a person if he wants a swimming pool in his backyard. He might say no, they're too complicated and expensive to maintain. And besides, it doesn't make financial sense because there's a community pool right down the road.

Makes sense, right?

But show the person the swimming pool in an ad that shows a whole family having fun, and he might salivate: "I've got to have one" or "If my neighbor gets one, then I'm going to get one too."

Did you ever think about the first guy who tried to explain the concept of beer to a banker who'd never tried it before?

"It's made from grain. It's sort of yellow with bubbles going through it. When you pour it too fast, it gets all foamy and spills all over the table. It tastes sort of bitter, and when you drink it you get dizzy and sometimes forget things."

It probably didn't work too well. Until our first brewmaker let the banker try it (they didn't have ads in those days), the banker didn't want it. The more he had, the more he wanted it. My God . . . this is good. The point is, it's easier to sell a product that one can see and taste and empathize with than to sell a naked idea.

Show people things they might want and suggest reasons they might want them. Then listen to the choices they make. Use interactive consumer groups or focus groups (or whatever name is trendy these days) to round up your target audience. They're a great deal more convenient than Abigail's method of attaching flowers to people on airplanes.

The basic premise of interactive consumer groups is simple.

▷ Gather potential customers in a room.
▷ Present stimuli to make them react.
▷ Listen to what they say.

In a group setting, consumers—business consumers too—will tell you anything if you ask the right way and make them react. They'll tell you where your product is lacking and where it's strong. They'll tell you who your competitors are. In the case of some businesses, they'll spell out secret dealings they have with not-so-ethical suppliers. Ask the right way and use the right stimuli and consumers will tell you what they're willing to pay for an item and where they'll get the money to pay for it. Most of all, they'll tell you their wants and needs and whether your product or positioning will satisfy them. That's what you want to hear.

As simple as interactive groups are, they can be abused. Marketers sometimes say, "We ran two focus groups, and the people liked the product." That's not how you should use consumer groups. Marketers should find out why the respondents liked the product, whether they would buy the product, and how your offering can be made into a more viable selling proposition. Successful focus groups are not about analysis, they're about making decisions.

What does *liking* a product mean? It could mean that the respondents are too embarrassed to tell the moderator the product is a dud. It could mean that they would like someone to give it to them as a gift (which they would never use). Saying that they like a product usually means that they are neutral. The idea doesn't turn them off, but it doesn't turn them on either. It's not bad enough to repel them, but that doesn't mean they are going to buy it.

It's not enough to get consumers to say that they like a product or service. The goal is to have consumers make an emotional commitment from the stimuli you bring in and the products they represent. Stimuli can be more than faux ads. They can be package prototypes, sales material, even your competitors' material—anything that might elicit a reaction.

One research company started off its focus group questioning for a travel product by asking why the respondents take vacations and how they choose their particular travel destinations. There are so many psychological factors that go into a vacation that even the vacationers can't pinpoint them. But if you show them stimuli that they identify with, they'll say, "Yeah, that's why I go." Don't ask consumers what they want. They'll all say they want their own little hut in Tahiti, all expenses paid. Instead, show them what they can have and force them to make choices.

Groups will also tell you when it's time to rethink a strategy and cut your losses. Recently a large grain company ran groups for a proposed cereal. At the end of the groups, the respondents were shown a commercial for the cereal. The response from eight groups was unanimous.

"Great commercial."

"Super, it really communicated a strong message."

"Wonderful—the imagery was fantastic."

"Wow, that's strong."

The agency was delighted—until a follow-up question was asked: "Would you buy the cereal based on this commercial?"

The answer was equally unequivocal: "No way."

"Why not?" was the moderator's response.

"That's not me in the commercial."

"I don't see myself as a driven hunk, like the guy lifting weights."

The commercial was well produced, but it never struck an emotional chord with consumers. It was fun to watch, but the message spoke to the wrong people.

Using Consumer Feedback

This can be called the "what if" reactive route to product and marketing success. You keep changing your product and selling proposition and ask your target audience:

▷ What if we *did* this—would you buy the product?

▷ What if the product *looked* like this—would you buy the product?

▷ What if we *said* this—would you buy the product?

Your variables include your positioning, your target market, and just about every aspect of your product. The process involves stimulating consumers with your product's putative messages and learning their buying preferences from their gut-level reactions to the stimuli. It is an evolutionary process that is built totally on consumer reaction.

The premise is simple: You dig for emotional biases and use this information to create new product and positioning alternatives. This process will also uncover marketing weaknesses or problems in the field so that you can make corrections. Consumers will be none too sparing when they attack your company or product. Don't take it too personally. The results, as unpalatable as they may be to the weak-kneed manager, will supply the necessary information for the development of a more effective and efficient marketing program. They can also lead you to a better business mission because the information comes directly from the people you will be trying to sell to.

The method starts off with theory (a fancy word for guess-work) and evolves into key findings. At the end of a project, you will have synthesized strong, winning, advertisable products and positionings. These can be readily implemented in the market-place because you know that your products and strategies have struck a targetable nerve. Moreover, these concepts are ready to use. They will have been developed from expressed consumer needs and tested to make sure that they met these needs.

Tools For Getting Into Consumers' Hearts

Tool 1: Real-World "Faux" Advertising Concepts

Now, not only do you not clumsily attach roses to people who step off airplanes, you also don't produce commercials for possible products or positionings as your advertising agency would like you to do. It would be great, but it's too expensive and time-consuming. In place of commercials, use concept boards. Every board and every component of the boards is a "what if" situation.

Create actual full-color ads (in layout form—don't hire an expensive photographer) for hypothetical products or services. Then present them to target consumers, not to find winning ads but to discern true motivation in a real-world setting. Here are two examples. Although the material was produced in color, it is shown here in black and white (Figure 3-1).

Don't use white card concepts like the one in Figure 3-2. (The concept is real, by the way, and the company that used it bit the dust.) White card boards don't elicit an emotional response. There's no motivating trigger. Unfortunately, this is the kind of material that's usually brought to interactive groups. It's bland, dull, and mind-numbing. It's fascinating that an advertising agency that would never present to its clients material that did not look as if it had been rendered by Michelangelo won't think twice about foisting slipshod concepts on unwitting groups of consumers.

Your ads should have the positioning built in. Ads are twentieth-century communication. They're what people respond to every day of their lives. If you can't create a simple ad around your product on a board, you won't be able to communicate the benefits to consumers in the real world. If you can't communicate your idea simply and convincingly, you don't have a product.

Study the concept boards in Figure 3-1. They include:

▷ The product, fully packaged
▷ Possible physical benefits
▷ Possible emotional benefits
▷ Lifestyle imagery
▷ Possible product names

These add up to your product's positioning.

This brings us to a key question that for some reason often befuddles marketing managers. How do you separate the product from the positioning? The answer: You don't. Consumers don't separate the product from the positioning, so why should

(text continues on page 52)

Figure 3-1. Sample of concept boards.

[A]

(continues)

Figure 3-1. *(continued)*

[B]

INTRODUCING

High Image
Moisturizing
Contact Lens Care
System

Helps prevent the wrinkles that occur around your eyes

*Incorporates a unique blend of
natural and scientific ingredients
to provide your lenses with the
ultimate in cleanliness, and your eyes
with the ultimate in moisturizers.*

with
SPECIAL FORMULA...
moisturizer
eye makeup
cleaning and
disinfecting
solution

Figure 3-2. The "usual" concept board (which doesn't work very well).

INTRODUCING A NEW ALL-PURPOSE, DISINFECTING CLEANER THAT DEEP CLEANS BEAUTIFULLY AND LEAVES A LONG-LASTING, MOUNTAIN-FRESH SCENT THAT'S RIGHT FOR EVERY ROOM IN THE HOUSE.

Not only does this new all purpose cleaner smell great, it cuts through dirt, grease and grime quickly and easily. Disinfects throughly, too. Eliminates disease and odor causing household germs by the millions.

This new product smells as wholesome as all outdoors. It's crisp, clean, mountain-fresh scent is right for every room. Tomorrow, you'll still enjoy its breezy freshness throughout the house.

Non-toxic, so you know it's safe to use in the kitchen, the nursery, sickrooms and around pets.

Best of all, this new cleaning formula replaces the need for a separate cleaner for the kitchen, the bathroom and floors. Now, one formula does it all.

you? In the store, consumers look at the product, the packaging, and the positioning as a complete unit. If the respondents want to buy your product because the name is cute, go with it. Any part of your product can function as a consumer hook. Make the consumer group a microcosm of the store experience.

Each concept board—and each component part of each concept board—is a trigger to unleash the minds and emotions of consumers. It doesn't matter whether consumers react to the whole selling proposition on the board or to an individual part of the concept board, as long as they react spontaneously, the way they do in the real world.

An emotional foundation can make even so-called parity products and low-interest products special. When you find an interesting hook, it makes your product seem special—even when it's only slightly different from any other product in the store. You'll also be amazed at how much consumer excitement you can generate in a low-interest or supersaturated product category. Way back when calculators were introduced, Texas Instruments separated its product from the mass of calculators with a simple device. Big green numbers and little rubber feet—it made a great jingle. It did nothing for the calculator's effectiveness, of course, but it was catchy to consumers, and Texas Instruments jumped to a leading market share.

For each concept, try to find a particular market or market premise. It's a trial-and-error approach. You try your ideas on consumers, and you make errors. What works, you leave alone. What doesn't work, you throw out or make better. There is no limit to the number of boards you can take to an interactive group provided they're well produced. Consumers have no problem digesting as many as thirty boards in a two-hour session and giving their reaction to each. In the supermarket, consumers are bombarded by over 10,000 products. They still gravitate to the one that fits their needs.

The sin is *not* developing enough ideas—*not* running the gamut of human emotions. When you run the emotional gamut, you'll uncover unpleasant emotions too. That's okay, because once you solve the unpleasantness, you can create a marketing opportunity. A product can be hated but still bought. Consumers despised the name Bully for the successful toilet bowl cleaner but admitted that cleaning the toilet bowl "bullied" them, so it was a good name.

As mentioned in the previous chapter, Toilet Duck took the opposite tack by adding elements of novelty and whimsy to the toilet-cleaning chore. Both toilet bowl cleaners are on target. There can be diverse consumer hooks in almost any category. The key is to develop a to-the-heart positioning that you *know* substantial groups of customers will embrace.

The opposite of love is not hate—it's indifference. If consumers are indifferent to your product, they won't buy it. If they love or even hate a product, at least they'll remember it.

Where Do the Ideas on the Boards Come From?

People ask how long it takes to write a concept board. For me, the answer is forty-seven years. Almost a half century of living has taught me everything I need to know about consumers, behavioral patterns, and marketing. Yeah, right! I'm wrong every time, at first. That's why you should develop a huge inventory of mini-experiments. The ideas should come from everyone—your secretary, your boss—even the people who clean your house. You'll find that once you come up with a starter group of ideas, your people will react to them and add more.

The creative inventory should expand to fit the project, with absolutely no limitations. Of course, it takes time to do a new ad for every idea, so one ad can function for a great many consumer premises. All it takes is a little piece of tape, some markers, and voilà—you have a new ad. Once again, these have been reproduced in black and white instead of color (Figure 3-3).

To force consumers to react, all creative work should be developed from all aspects of your products. Don't ask them if the product would look better in red, show them the product in red. Often what sounds good in theory looks just lousy when you finally make the product, and vice versa. I ran some groups on a new seafood dinner. I asked the consumers, more out of curiosity than anything else, if we should make the package black. Most consumers didn't like the idea at all. Then I showed consumers a mocked-up black package. Most of them quickly decided that black was their favorite color.

(text continues on page 57)

Figure 3-3. Same basic product, three positionings.

[A]

Introducing
Eye-Watch A.M.
for contact lenses

Two drops, first thing in the morning, can help your contact lenses feel better all day.

- Lubricates lenses.
- Helps remove nighttime protein build-up.
- Makes lenses feel fresh first thing in the morning.

The cycle starts the first thing in the morning. Your eyes are dry, so you rub them..which irritates them and makes you rub some more.

The result...contacts are uncomfortable all day.

New EyeWatch A.M. changes all that. Two drops first thing in the morning replaces natural tear levels in your eyes and helps remove deposits that form on your eyes overnight.

With EyeWatch A.M your eyes get off to a fresh start.

[B]

Introducing
Eye-Watch
for contact lenses

Two drops, first thing in the morning, can help your contact lenses feel better all day.

- Lubricates lenses.
- Helps remove nighttime protein build-up.
- Makes lenses feel fresh first thing in the morning.

The cycle starts the first thing in the morning. Your eyes are dry, so you rub them..which irritates them and makes you rub some more.

The result...contacts are uncomfortable all day.

New EyeWatch changes all that. Two drops first thing in the morning replaces natural tear levels in your eyes and helps remove deposits that form on your eyes overnight.

With EyeWatch your eyes get off to a fresh start.

(continues)

Figure 3–3. *(continued)*

[C]

Introducing

Eye-Watch P.M.

for contact lenses

Two drops in the early evening keeps lenses soft and comfortable all night.

Excellent for
tired eyes.

Delivers oxygen
to the eye to
prevent late evening
dryness.

Allows you to
wear lenses
longer.

Introducing Eye Watch P.M. It's a
revolutionary new contact lens drop
that actually releases vital and
comforting oxygen to your eyes.

EyeWatch P.M.'s special oxygen releasing
ingredients work as a gentle buffer and
help keep your eyes moist and your lenses
comfortable all night long.

You never know what the response to your concepts will be until you show them to consumers. Consumers' feelings and perceptions will always surprise you, especially when they differ from yours. Did you know that American Airlines gets loads of requests every year for the recipes for its airplane food? Consumer perceptions are not always right—but that's just my perception.

Tool 2: Consumer Groups That Identify Preferences and Your Target Market

Interactive consumer groups can also be used to find your target audience. Most projects start with a vision or speculation of who your target audience is. This may be right or wrong. As with your initial concept boards, choosing the initial group makeup involves a little guesswork and a little knowledge. Major factors to consider are the purchasers and the people who influence the purchase. Demographics and income levels are also important. While it's obvious that you should include pet owners if you're doing a study on a new pet food, whom you should include may not be so obvious for a fireplace product or a car. Whose emotional strings do you have to pull—the husband's or the wife's?

When a new toothpaste was developed for Colgate, an abundance of products and positionings for teenagers was created. They included products that spanned the gamut of teenage emotions. Several groups of teenagers were involved in the project, and many of the kids loved the concepts. Then they were asked the key question again: "Would you buy the product?" The response was a unanimous and resounding no. Even though these were typically independent teenagers, they trusted their mothers to make the toothpaste choice. When my kids and my relatives' kids went off to college, they all asked their mothers what kind of toothpaste they should buy. (At least they need us for something!)

Alternatives to Interactive Groups

Sometimes it's hard to bring in a concentrated number of people who may buy your product into a group. This can happen in a business-to-business situation where there are a relatively small number of customers scattered around the country. An alternative is to take your boards to the respondent's place of business and use the same stimulus-reaction game plan. Some marketers are put off by this. They say that businesspeople won't take the time or won't be honest. This is usually not the case. Businesspeople take pride in their expertise and like to show off. Just assure them that you are not trying to sell them anything, you just want them to help you make better products for their business. A trick to get respondents to talk to you is to fax them a letter in advance, stating your research purpose.

Tool 3: You and Your Marketing Crew

By the time you read a consumer-group report, it's secondhand information. Few reports can communicate the excitement the respondents show when they're in tune with an idea, and no report can make you as exasperated as you're going to feel when you see your pet idea blow up in your face. And make no mistake, this will happen to most of your ideas at first. Nothing beats sitting in the back room and learning firsthand how your ideas play or don't play.

Let's digress a little here and talk about poker playing. If you get nothing else from this book, at least you may be able to steal the pot at your next weekly game.

The conventional thinking is that a person who is bluffing will reveal the fact with nervous twitches and shaking. Gamblers call such body language "the tell." Observation shows the opposite. The shaker is the person who has what he or she considers a great hand. The person suspiciously eyes the other player's exposed card to see what chance there is to win. The person consciously questions whether or not to stay in the pot. The player is excited because he or she has a chance to win—and can almost taste it. His or her face shows that the person would love to ask questions, but obviously can't.

The bluffer, on the other hand, consciously reins in his or her emotions, because he or she knows the only chance is to bluff. The bluffer is uninterested in the other people's cards because he or she knows his or her hand is weak.

It's the same way in interactive groups. The people who want your product will ask questions and get excited. They'll tell you what's wrong with your concepts and what's right with them. The disinterested consumer will sit stoically like our bluffer, say that he or she likes the product, and hurry out to get the incentive money you pay for coming to the groups.

When you deal with consumers, it's the emotional outburst you want. You should hope that consumers care enough about the product to get truly excited. The concept boards may not be right yet, but something in there is turning the customers on— whether it's the name, the product, the visual, or even a word or two in the body copy.

It should be the concepts, not the moderator, that do the job of turning on the respondent. The moderator's job is to probe for loose ends in the concepts and also to tie in what the respondents are saying to the real world of marketing. In this technique, it is important to leave moderators somewhat unstructured in their approach. A good moderator will let the ads and the client's goals guide him or her at the group's own pace and interest.

The key in working with respondents is, don't ask them to theorize or intellectualize. Make them react, just as they do in the real world. Don't expect consumer participants to be marketing experts or to do a marketer's job. Let them be consumers. Force them to tell you what they want based on what they are seeing. Stimulate them with the proper concepts and they'll divulge their secrets in detail.

The concept board reactive approach creates a climate that opens the door to a much more dynamic interaction between people. Thinking becomes less linear and more diverse—some might even say chaotic. Individuals become more productive. The idea is not to narrow down your ideas, but to always expand your knowledge with new thinking based on how the consumers are responding.

But the response to each idea, whether good or bad, should lead you to insights about your marketing strategy and customer base. If you're developing a new product or business, you can take bankers and investors to your groups. You could, of course, furnish videotapes or transcripts, but nothing is as dramatic as being there. It's important to have people listening who are or will be emotionally involved in the project. They'll get turned on by the enthusiasm of the consumers. It's become an axiom that the major complainers on a project find ways to avoid attending groups. They're almost always the first to judge your findings wrong. Have a strict rule with your staff: If you weren't at the groups, you can't criticize the findings.

Build Your Insights

Those were the tools. Here's how to build your insights.

You should run groups wherever you expect to have a market. If you're thinking of a national product, you should hit geographically diverse areas. On the Colgate project, a toothpaste with calcium was offered.

In New York, they loved it. The Colgate team was excited.

Then, off to the Midwest—America's heartland. Consumers were skeptical. "How is the calcium going to soak into my teeth?" they asked. "Uh, oh," the Colgate team thought. "We're in trouble."

Finally, to Charlotte, North Carolina. "What's calcium?" the respondents asked. The product idea was shelved fast. Right after that, Procter & Gamble launched Gleem toothpaste with calcium. Paranoia set in. Had something been missed in the study? It hadn't. The product was a dud.

Yes, there will be wondering. You'll think that your answer was too simple. The key to the consumer's heart is almost always disarmingly simple. It's so simple that you'll try to make your product or message more complicated than it really is. Resist the urge to make constant improvements after your final groups—even if your consumer feedback goes against current marketing theory or your own preconceived notions. If consumers say they will buy your product, take them at their word.

Most projects need three rounds of consumers. Try to hold them about three weeks apart so that you have time to revise your creative output. If you don't have the luxury of that much time, that's okay too. Your program may work even better. A time-intensive program often gets better results than a long-drawn-out one. Time actually spent on a project expands to fit the time allotted for a project. An intense, concentrated program gets the adrenaline flowing. But no matter how you space out the time frames in your program, try to put in one- or two-day pause points. These are short periods for reflection in which you

can digest all that you have heard in your groups. It takes time to make sense when you're speaking to the heart.

The Plan: Putting It All Together

The following is a basic time flow plan. The average time it takes to develop key consumer-driven strategies, new products, or motivational insights is three to four months. If there is a time pinch, the research can be completed in six weeks or less.

First Wave: Initial Concept Development

Use two or three consumer groups.

Objective: Identify broad-scale areas that have potential. Eliminate red flags. Get a preliminary reading of your market and consumer composition.

At this first step, you can let your mind go free. Because nothing has been shown to consumers, no one can be wrong. Your faux ads can be developed about almost anything remotely related to the product. Try packaging variations, copy lines, product formulations—anything that makes reasonable sense to just about anyone. This is also a great time to try out your management's pet ideas. Even if they're bombs, you can honestly say that you tried them. At this time you should have started with a totally blank slate—an open mind. These initial concepts are directional indicators—core ads. They are starting points that may or may not be modified or rejected at later stages. All concepts, of course, should have an emotional viewpoint built in.

Your recruiting is also very general. You should be careful not to whittle down your target market too soon. You want to speak with different market segments and be careful to listen to what turns whom on.

Second Wave: Creative and Concept Reevaluation

Use two or three interactive groups. The goal is additional concept development and evolution.

Objectives: Expand on areas that have merit. Further define areas of opportunity.

The original ads will be modified and new ads, based on your findings in the first groups, will be added to the creative inventory.

The goal of the second phase is to get more down to earth with your concepts based on consumer feedback. What worked in the first groups is left alone to serve as a benchmark. What didn't work you either throw out or revise. New concepts must beat your best concepts from the first group. Now, it's natural to want to whittle down your concepts to a more manageable number, but that's counterproductive. Because of what you have learned from the first groups, you may have even more concepts (Figure 3-4).

Third Wave: Continuing Creative Modification and Refinement

Use two or three interactive groups.

Figure 3-4. How concepts evolve.

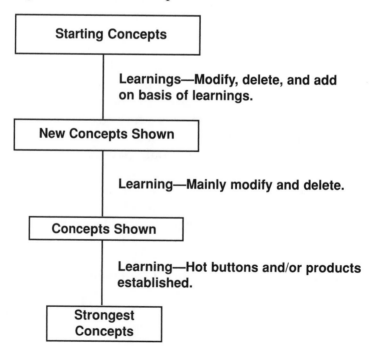

Objectives: Continue the evolutionary process. Identify the specific consumer hot buttons and target market. Optimize concepts and consumer triggers.

By the third round of groups, you know what your product is, and who's going to buy it. Almost always, by the end of the groups, you'll find out something sickening: The solution to the problem was obvious. The answer is always obvious after the work is done. The keys to consumers' hearts are simple—once you find your target market's hot button.

Don't Use Your Advertising Agency

Even the best-motivated advertising agencies have trouble with this kind of research. Many creative ad people resent having to do the down and dirty work of speaking with consumers, even though these are the people who will actually buy the product. They find it demeaning for geniuses like themselves. The thought process of the creative hack goes something like this: "If the ad doesn't motivate the consumer, it's the consumer's fault for not understanding it."

The agency, despite its "sincere" devotion to the project, has trouble justifying the investment. It can't put its more talented creative people on the project because that would take too much time away from media work, which generates agency income. Also, there is no incentive. Agency creative people are always building their portfolios, and concept work does not generate compelling four-color print ads or commercials.

So agencies assign the work to juniors who have neither the skills nor the incentive to do a bang-up job. Agencies exist primarily to create and place media campaigns. We'll get into how to make your agency and your advertising work harder and more effectively in Chapter 9.

Now Use the Results

It takes intelligence to use intelligence. All the reports in the world won't do any good unless someone actually uses them.

Good marketers take the time to go out to the real world of people and listen to what they say. Discipline comes into play when you use these findings even when they contradict your preconceived notion.

I don't know how Abigail's and Lieutenant Smith's lives went after their meeting, but by exploring each other's hearts, they probably got off to a good start.

In Chapter 6, we'll discuss how this method—with a few variations—can be used to create new products and marketing opportunities and dramatically increase the odds of a successful launch.

▶ *4*

Staking Your Claim to Your Target Market: The to-the-Heart Mission Statement

It was destined to become the biggest company in its category, with one of the most recognized brand names on the planet. Although the product was given many awards and proclaimed the best of its kind, it was not this that made it the success it was soon to become.

It was a commitment to a certain principle by an entrepreneur that made the product so successful.

The entrepreneur behind the company was Eberhard Anheuser. In the mid-1800s Anheuser and his son-in-law, Adolphus Busch, teamed up to brew and sell a new beer from a brewery that Anheuser had acquired as payment of a debt. Anheuser was the businessman. Busch was, well, a gregarious sort with limited business experience. Making beer was not his talent. Making friends was.

Busch had a simple approach to sales. Anheuser thought it was too simple. "Our business is not just making beer," Busch would say. "Making friends is our business."

So making friends became the Anheuser-Busch mission. Those five little words, "making friends is our business," quickly set Anheuser-Busch apart from the competition. Of course, the beer—Budweiser—was of high quality, but Busch always said, "It's not beer. Our friends are our business."

To this day, Budweiser is sold as a product for conviviality. Anheuser-Busch has remained true to its beginnings and true to its mission statement. To the Anheuser-Busch founders, this was more than just an empty-headed advertising slogan, it was a way of doing business. It was a way to get into the customer's heart.

A clear, customer-based mission statement is vital to a focused business, division, or product. That's why this chapter is devoted to what amounts to a mere handful of words. The key is to find out what your customers want and build your mission statement around satisfying their needs. A concise, consumer-driven mission statement is a stepping-stone to winning the hearts and minds of consumers.

A mission statement is a superbrief proclamation of your business intent—your business plan written on the head of a pin. It's as brief and pithy as a classified ad. If you can't describe your mission in a few sentences, then you don't have a clear handle on your customers' needs. The mission statement functions as the heart and soul of your marketing strategy and provides a vivid checkpoint to make sure your product or service stays focused. As statesman Benjamin Disraeli said, "The secret to success is consistency of purpose."

Strangely, most companies operate without a mission statement. They don't search into the hearts of their customers before they come up with their grandiose business plans. This is like building a house without a blueprint. Most businesses do have some sort of plan to show bankers and to please the accountants and stockholders, but few have a clear-cut mission statement engineered to win the hearts and minds of their customers.

In *start-up companies*, managers are so busy that they think they have no time for a formal mandate.

In *established companies*, even if someone had the forethought to develop a mission statement, it is usually hidden away in a closet.

Downtrending companies are so wrapped up in creating sales in order to pay bills, that they think they have no time to worry about a mission statement.

When companies do formulate a mission statement, most of them define their mission in product terms or technological terms. The mission goal should be people-oriented, not product-oriented. No matter how special your product is, you don't have a company unless someone wants to buy your product. Your products are going to change over the lifespan of your business, but your customers are always going to have needs that must be met. The world can go on without your product, but your company can't go on without your customers.

A mission statement should be written down, for a simple reason: Sometimes you forget it. In the day-to-day running of a business, it's easy to forget what you're setting out to do in the first place.

The makers of CD-ROMs, media that can hold tons of computer information and large computer games, are in serious trouble. Sales are slow, and many companies have shut down or laid off employees. That's because there is a lack of software products that sufficiently arouse consumers. Because there are so many bland offerings, a new product gets only a few weeks to prove itself in the marketplace—if it makes it onto the shelves at all. CD-ROM producers have forgotten that their business mission is not to sell plastic disks, but rather to generate games and programs to titillate the imagination and amuse. The CD-ROM is only a *holder* of fun and mystery—essentially the envelope the fun comes in. There is little market for the carrier of the message.

Enlightened Companies Always Put the Customer First

Here's a product-based mission statement for a discount department store:

> *We're in business to sell a wide variety of products to people and earn profits for our stockholders.*

What does that say? Nothing. What is there that leads to action? Nothing. Of course you're in business to make money!
Here's the mission statement for Wal-Mart:

To provide a range of products that deliver value to Middle America.

This brief sentence says everything. It offers consumers emotional and practical benefits. On the emotional side, people are comfortable in knowing they're getting a good deal. On the practical side, Wal-Mart's execution of the mission statement means that consumers really are getting a good deal. The statement also targets the customers: Middle America.

You can build a huge business on that simple mission statement. And that's what Sam Walton, Wal-Mart's founder, did. The premise is so strong that Wal-Mart's managers have been able to keep the company running profitably since his death. The mission statement is part of Walton's legacy.

A formal mission statement encourages managers to forge ahead systematically. It helps the managers focus on environmental business changes and prepare for sudden developments.

The very search for a mission statement will lead to greater productivity if you get everyone involved. Very often—in most companies, actually—divisions are at cross purposes. For instance, many companies have new venture groups. Their mandate is to create new businesses, but when the venture group asks for funding, the request is usually shot down for some vague reason, such as the new business not being a good fit. If there is no all-encompassing consumer mission, how can anyone judge whether a new business is a good fit?

Marketing tells R&D to make what it can sell. R&D, in turn, gripes that marketing can't sell what R&D makes. Hey, guys, you're supposed to be on the same side.

A mission statement should integrate all departments. Get all the key groups involved in creating and executing the mission statement. This eliminates many conflicts between departments because everyone knows what goals are to be set, and that leads to these goals being met.

The mission statement guides every department, especially marketing, to achieve your corporate goals. A to-the-heart mission statement inspires as well as directs. Mission substatements keep your divisions highly targeted.

Here's a corporate mission statement for a cereal company:

To provide American consumers with the knowledge that they're getting a nutritious breakfast every day.

Here's a substatement for the company's new product division:

To provide interesting new products and choices that ensure consumers a day's worth of energy in every bowl of our cereal.

A clear mission statement helps keep your organization focused. When management senses that the organization is drifting and getting away from your customer's needs, they can refer back to the mission statement.

Four Requisites for Your Mission Statement

1. *It should be real-world-oriented.* It's nice to dream about your company over a few beers, but it's more important to make your mission statement practical and workable—and in tune with your prospective customer. Realistic goals cannot be set unless your mission statement is feasible.

2. *It should be specific.* Making a mission statement sound like an advertising slogan is tempting, but an empty slogan is like one of those trendy motivational speakers. It pumps you up for a few minutes, then the feeling is gone. Your business mission statement should contain exact goals and explain how you are going to meet those goals. You can be specific by identifying exactly what consumer needs you're going to be satisfying and how you're going to satisfy them. Her Interactive, a computer software company, found through research that girls ages thirteen through sixteen were not playing computer games as much as boys because they did not like the same games boys did. Boys liked the shoot-'em-up, conquer-the-aliens games and other action titles. Girls wanted more emotion. So Her Interactive created a mission statement focused on developing software specifically for teenage girls and found a niche for itself in the market.

The Anheuser-Busch mission statement doesn't go into too many details, but it specifically governs how the company advertises and markets its products.

3. *It should be flexible.* Being flexible means you're ready to change to meet your customer's needs. It means you can change strategies to meet the competitive conditions and change your ways of doing business to meet changing consumer needs.

Go back to the Anheuser-Busch statement. As the company's customers change, new ways of "making friends" can be developed. The successful mission statement creates new opportunities by broadening the company's executional tools.

Flexibility also means having an expansive vision for the future. Intuit created Quicken software for the home computer market and could have been content to handle just the consumer end of the software business. But Intuit gracefully satisfied other markets, going into computer banking and developing new business-to-business markets for its products—and creating new products for its markets.

4. *It should be simple.* There is a tendency to make a mission statement complicated by adding one sentence after another. You shouldn't. Brevity makes all the difference between a focused strategy and a diffused one. Remember, the Ten Commandments were written on two plaques.

Supermarketing: Wired to Success

No more "What's your sign?" The new topic of party conversation is, "What's your AOL screen name?" In the past two years, America Online has grown from 350,000 members to more than 6 million members.

America Online started as a simple message service for Apple computers, but its strict adherence to making on-line communication accessible to the "technologically challenged" gave it license to venture into new areas. It now dwarfs IBM-driven Prodigy and the one-time market leader CompuServe.

America Online is seen as cutting edge, whereas Prodigy is considered old, dull, and stale.

The difference is in the way the two services were positioned in their formative stages. Prodigy was conceived of as an information service, America Online as a communications facilitator.

America Online was a new medium where people could meet other people, stay informed, buy products, and learn new things.

The company was the first to make its service user-friendly, so that people with no knowledge of computers could communicate freely and easily. Steve Case, CEO of America Online, talks about his company as a community, rather than an on-line service.

People meet on-line, talk on-line, and even get married. (You can't do that on-line—yet.) They console one another via computer and congratulate one another through the same medium.

Case talks about the six Cs that make up his mission statement: content, community, context, connectivity, commerce, and cost. All growth has centered on improving these elements.

By the way, my screen name is Newmex. What's yours?

Look Hard at Your Mission Statement—Often

While the mission statement is for long-term growth, it should be looked at annually to make sure it's meeting your needs and responding to changes in the marketplace.

A natural skin care store, The Body Shop, had a mission goal that was so strong, the store advertised it:

To sell natural products that you can feel good about and are not tested on animals.

Recently, a magazine alleged that some of the company's products had, indeed, been tested on animals. Although The Body Shop was eventually cleared, the negative publicity could have caused untold harm. That's why you have to continually look at your mission statement and update it as conditions come about that play on your customer's psyche.

A new mission statement can also help you reinvent the company. This is called a paradigm shift—changing the way you look at things, adjusting your business focus. Paradoxically, this is equally important in a stagnating old-line industry and a high-tech company where consumer needs evolve in a nanosecond. You may be bringing a glorious new computer or computer peripheral to market and find that someone has beaten you. When that happens, it's time to rethink your plans and go on to something more profitable, or sell your product to a different market. The people who made WordPerfect found that the market for word processors was saturated. Since the company had no alternative plans, it was forced to agree to be acquired by Corel, another computer software company.

The following tells about mistakes of omission made by a company that lost its way because it had no preemptive mission.

American Cyanamid owned Shulton (aftershave and colognes) and Pine-Sol (cleaning products). American Cyanamid's management was adamant about not marketing a new product or line extension unless it had some kind of physical hook. This is tough in the fragrance and cleaning businesses. American Cyanamid ignored the emotional needs of its customers. This caused both Shulton and Pine-Sol to flatline in the growth category.

Procter & Gamble bought both product lines and immediately created highly successful new products and line extensions based on emotional attributes. American Cyanamid could have achieved the same success with the brands if it had learned about the brands' emotional equities, built a strong mission statement for the brands, and executed the statement.

The lack of a strong emotional statement also sank a major new product for American Cyanamid. It launched an underarm deodorant that came in a dispenser that was new to consumers. The advertising talked only about the new dispenser and ignored the emotionality that is so necessary to the deodorant category. The product died. By the way, so did American Cyanamid. The do-little company was eventually bought by American Home Products.

Creating Your Mission Statement

A clear mission statement functions as a laser beam, focusing on the key aspects that can make your business grow. It should answer several vital questions.

What Is Your Business?

Of course you know what you make or sell and eat and breathe, but many executives get caught up in the day-to-day running of their businesses. They lose sight of the corporate mission, which is usually more than just pleasing the stockholders. Deciding on your business is not as cut and dried as it sounds.

John White is president of Hudson Foods, a poultry producer in Rogers, Arkansas. Most chicken producers would say that their corporate goal is to grow and sell chickens. That's the product-oriented mission. It may be technically right, but that's not where the money is. Mr. White takes a larger view: the consumer "to the heart" vision. He says that the company's mission is to deliver good-tasting products to satisfy his customers' needs for protein. So he has come up with fajita kits, new chicken products, and a variety of fun, value-added meals. All of these products elicit higher prices from consumers.

The beef people could take some lessons from Mr. White. Beef purveyors think their business is selling dead cows and insist on the "that's the way we've always done it" commodity way of doing business. They need a clearer understanding of the consumers' emotional needs. Once they find those needs, they can create and execute a clear mission statement. This will create higher demand and lead to higher prices for their products.

American Express defines its business not as charge cards, but as helping consumers manage their financial resources.

Tom's of Maine (a natural hygiene products company) says, "Back in the sixties, you were either for business or for the environment. You didn't know you could be for both. At Tom's, our mission is to provide people with effective products that are fun and don't harm the environment."

This is an effective, simple play to the heart.

Deciding on your mission statement requires looking at the big picture. An advertising agency might say it's in the business of producing ads and brochures. That's not the customer-oriented way of looking at things. The agency's mission should be creating business for its clients and providing a comfort level for these clients.

A bookbinding company thought it was in the business of binding books for its customers. It thought all of its customers were after the lowest price. Meeting these cost objectives dried up profits. Then the company rethought its business and wrote a mission statement. It concluded that its business was guiding customers through the entire publishing maze. This guidance saved the customers money and made the binder a source to be relied on. Profits skyrocketed.

A fireplace company spent a year trying to find out whether it was selling a new kind of fuel or a new fireplace appliance. Sure, it was selling heat. But the consumer was buying romance. It sounds like semantics, but when the company finally created the mission statement, a whole new product category opened up. It's the classic case of the chicken and the egg. Are you selling expensive widgets because you can make them, or are you satisfying your customers' need for widgets? If you find out you're satisfying customers, than you can add to your product line by solving even more problems.

What Does Your Customer Want From You?

Don't deliver what you can make because that's what is currently available. Find out what your customers want and create a mission statement that will deliver those wants. A strong marketer takes the path of least consumer resistance. That path coincides exactly with how your customers think about themselves. Do your customers consider themselves upscale or more down-to-earth? Do they consider themselves conservative or trendsetters? The Mazda Miata was a sports car invented for the midlife crisis. Mazda knew its customers intimately. The mission was to design a car that harkened back to a period when people remembered life as being gay and carefree.

Tom's knows that its customers are naturally oriented. They shop in both supermarkets and health food stores and are prepared to pay extra for a product they perceive as natural. So Tom's tells them what they want to hear. It's manifested in just about everything, from the mission statement to the product's package.

Customers and their product choices will evolve to meet the changing marketplace, and it is the job of your mission statement to ensure that your company keeps up with this evolution.

Fred Smith had a notion that he could get any package from any point in the country to any other point in the country in one day. He had a plan—a mission that he never lost sight of. Smith went out and built Federal Express.

Federal Express promotes its product line based on its simple mission statement of fast, secure overnight delivery. Everything flows from the mission of getting a client's product to the destination when the client wants it. When other companies, even (yipes) the inept U.S. Post Office, challenged his idea, he came up with new twists, which he applied as soon as competitors came near. Federal Express now has a whole laundry list of marketing strategies that keeps other companies continually guessing—and the consumer continually satisfied.

Federal Express uses the hot button of "security" in developing package-tracking products that let the user know exactly where a package is at all times. Your package may be somewhere in a Fedex plane over Walla Walla, Washington, but at least you know it's there.

The mission statement laid the groundwork for short-term and long-term success.

How Focused Are You With Your Assets?

A mission statement can also help you focus on where your equities should be expanded. Many companies have made acquisitions and developed new products that were outside of their sphere of equity. Gerber developed a line of dinner entrees for adults that was a huge business failure. Sears got involved with Prodigy, which drained its cash resources. Even Anheuser-Busch had to jettison its Eagle snack business because it was too far afield from its beer equity.

Using the Mission Statement

Now that you have this small collection of words, what do you do with it? Of course, you could bronze it, post it in your reception room, and forget about it, as many companies do. But it should really drive your advertising, your promotion, and even your supplier relations.

Here's another example of a marketing opportunity gone wrong because of a lack of a clear mission statement.

Charlie's Specialty Meats makes a number of products. The one the company is most excited about is Partially Deboned Chicken and Stuffing. That's the actual name—as romantic as it sounds. The product is a whole chicken with an assortment of rice dressings.

If Charlie's, out of Franklin, Louisiana, had used a little marketing savvy and packaging help, this could have been a real winner.

But Charlie's is struggling. It obviously doesn't have a mission statement that it uses, nor does it have any psychological hook. Customers have to stumble over the product and create their own uses. There is also little reason for a supermarket to stock the product because there is no salesmanship on the package. This could have all been avoided if Charlie's had looked at its market, created a mission goal, and named and promoted the product with a Share of Heart that played off the mission statement.

Advertising

Your advertising should flow from your mission statement, not vice versa. All advertising should be based on executions derived from the statement. Your advertising will work more effectively and be more on target when you explain to the agency the entire corporate mission and how the advertising creative product should fit in.

Promotion

All promotion should likewise play off the mission statement. Besides increasing short-term sales, all promotion should reinforce the basic mission goal. McDonald's and other fast-food companies take a lot of flack for spending their ad dollars on toys, trinkets, and contests at the expense of hard-core image advertising. But every promotion contributes to McDonald's long-term mission of being thought of as family restaurants.

A good mission statement can help you develop cross promotions and help you license the good feeling your products provide. Nabisco has taken SnackWell's "good taste, low fat" feeling and licensed it to a number of companies with "good for you" products.

The Product Mix

It's relatively easy to cull your products and develop new ones once you have developed a mission statement. It's like sculpting a statue of an elephant: Just chisel away all the parts that don't look like an elephant. If your products don't enhance the mission statement or aren't enhanced by the mission statement, either fix them or get rid of them.

Working With Suppliers

When you share your mission statement with suppliers or work with them on developing the mission statement, they will become more helpful. That's because they'll know the whole story, rather than just bits and pieces.

Recently, a company that was developing a new dough product called an R&D development company to help.

Instead of saying to the R&D company, "This is what we want," the whole marketing mission was discussed: "This is our mission; we'd like your team to help us fulfill it." The R&D company, looking at the whole picture, suggested things that never would have been thought of if it had been given only the partial picture or a typical "make-the-product" scenario.

Adding Life to Your Employees

J. Barry Golliday of Information Resources adds one more point: A mission statement should also have meaning to employees, for they are the people who are going to execute the statement. A mission statement should both inspire and challenge employees. Employees want to be challenged to work better. As mentioned in Chapter 3, people cherish intrinsic rewards. Unless your people care about your business and are a key part of your mission statement, your business objectives will probably not be fulfilled. Employees like being part of a growing firm. It's exciting having a major part in the birth of a success. Golliday also mentioned that a good mission statement should appeal to the stockholders too, but if you create a to-the-heart mission statement and follow through on it, your sales will make your investors very happy.

The Corporate Vision

The mission statement may be just a handful of words, but it describes the entire corporate vision in shorthand terms. It helps keep you and your departments fully focused on what needs to be done and why it needs to be done.

A strong mission statement plays to the hearts of your ultimate consumers and functions as a guide to achieving product and corporate goals. Why should a mission statement be written down? Simple. Because sometimes you forget it.

▷ 5

Developing the Marketing Strategy

The Santa Fe Natural Tobacco Company markets additive-free natural cigarettes, called American Spirit. Cigarette marketing is a minefield of government regulations and antismoking prejudices. The market is dominated by billion-dollar multinational conglomerates that can swat a potential competitor as swiftly as they can extinguish a match in a glassful of water.

Launching a new cigarette under these conditions seems a bit (to be polite) ludicrous. But Robin Sommers, president of Santa Fe Natural Tobacco Company, likes being an ash flick on the cuff of the corporate egomaniacs.

Once he had identified and explored the competition, Sommers found his massive competitors to be emotionally dysfunctional. More important, because of the *Zeitgeist* of the times, he could exploit the dysfunctions. The situation was as follows:

1. The major players in the cigarette industry were, and still are, in a fight to the death with the government for their right to pollute the lungs of Americans without discriminating as to race, sex, or creed. They were equal opportunity destroyers.

Sommers knew that they were distracted. They would ignore the bite of a marketing mosquito (which Sommers was). That made them vulnerable to a new cigarette launch, particularly if it was targeted to a new audience that they had not identified.

2. Existing cigarettes were loaded with additives, essentially making them nicotine delivery machines. But manufacturers

could not admit this to the general public. Sommers' product was additive-free. If the cigarette manufacturers fought Sommers on the additive issue, they would be forced to admit to millions of smokers that their own cigarettes were loaded with chemicals.

3. Cigarette companies were loathed by multitudes of Americans, so many counterculturish people were thrilled to buy an alternative cigarette. They rationalized the cigarettes as being healthier than conventional smokes.

4. Cigarette companies were large and unwieldy beasts that were not able to market nimbly to a tiny niche market. They were used to dealing with hundreds of millions of dollars. The comparatively small amount of money that Santa Fe Natural Tobacco could earn would hardly pay for a dinner and a hotel room for the major tobacco companies' lawyers.

Taking all these emotional and marketing issues into consideration, Sommers knew he had a winner. He would effectively develop his own niche market. Sommers could tackle the cigarette industry head on. Well, not exactly head on. He could sort of slip into their deep pockets for loose change.

There was one factor that Sommers wasn't sure about: pride. How would the corporate megalomaniacs react to this person taking market share away from them?

Emotions Drive Corporate America, Too

Yes, companies make many of their marketing decisions based on dollars and cents, but they also react to motivational variables. Cigarette manufacturers had to decide emotionally whether to ignore the minuscule bite that Robin Sommers might inflict or gather their resources to fumigate the whole bog. Corporate pride and esprit de corps is an important part of company make-up. Some marketing companies actually get angry when another company invades their turf—sometimes irrationally so.

So Sommers took all steps necessary to avoid rousing these sleeping or inattentive giants.

He advertised in media the majors had never heard about, such as the *Utne Reader* and other counterculture but upscale magazines. He offered free samples by mail and advertised for distributors and customers in the same ad. He made personal visits to prospective retailers. He made his selling trips so often that he became a professional guest.

He now has an established business.

Sommers' product actually sells five times instead of the four mandatory times (on the shelf, at the checkout counter, in use, and after it runs out) mentioned in the first chapter.

▷ In ads, it is obvious that American Spirit is not like traditional cigarettes.

▷ In the store, its Native American imagery is unlike that of any other cigarette. The product is also more expensive, so smokers perceive it as something special.

▷ Because it is somewhat of an impulse product, its very uniqueness makes it pass the consumer's cut list.

▷ In use, the product lasts longer than traditional cigarettes, reinforcing the all-natural claim.

▷ And, after trying the product and comparing it to traditional cigarettes, the customers want more—and they tell their friends about it.

Marketing to the heart works the same way for small players as for large players. And it's really not a function of how much money one has. It can be just as easy to blow a $20,000 stake, as hundreds of would-be entrepreneurs do each week, as it is to blow $500 million, as RCA did with its Selectavision videodisk player.

Smaller entrepreneurs-to-be seem to work extra hard at separating themselves from cash. As a rule, they simply don't do their homework. They only think they do. They ask friends and family what they think of a new business venture. Friends and family politely say, "That's a very nice idea, honey. Why don't you eat your dinner." They want to be supportive even when it's not in their own best interests. Alternatively, friends may say, "It's not really a good idea," but the entrepreneur plugs on nonetheless, thinking, "What do they know?" Unless you're asking for money, it's wise to adopt the don't ask, don't tell attitude with regard to your business venture with people you know. They'll give you emotional biases that you don't need.

But you do need a strategy—one that will take you into the hearts of your customer. Like a mission statement, it should be written.

Push-Button Marketing to the Heart

Think of a marketing strategy as a collection of buttons on your computer. Each button, or key, triggers certain events. If you press the keys at random, eventually you'll come up with a word. But if you press the keys in a predetermined order, you'll come up with the exact word you want—one that has meaning and substance; one that will get you to the heart of your business.

Spending time at the beginning of your marketing foray in the planning stages (steps 1 through 3) will save you money when you actualize the plan (steps 4 and 5) and get you that much closer to success.

The keys are:

1. Identify.
2. Segment.
3. Focus.
4. Attack (adapt and adopt).
5. Evolve.

See Figure 5-1.

The Identify Key

Marketing an existing or new product is an opportunistic profession. But marketing opportunities don't reach out and bite you on the behind. You have to probe for them. Marketing is a process of identifying things and pouncing on them. "Seek and ye shall find" is the biblical shorthand for research. Many marketers and entrepreneurs are so excited by their product, they think the world is just waiting for it. But when you do your homework in advance, you'll find flaws that you can correct before you spend big bucks or look foolish to your corporate colleagues.

There are a great many things you have to identify to make a marketing foray successful. It's like a scavenger hunt for clues

Figure 5-1. Push-button marketing to the heart.

◯ **Identify**	Product. Positioning. Consumer Motivations. Competition.
◯ **Segment**	Heartfelt segmentation. Target your audience.
◯ **Focus**	Concentrate your resources on your target.
◯ **Attack**	Adapt and adopt.
◯ **Evolve**	Change to stay ahead of your competition and on top of your market.

to a puzzle. The difference is, as you find these clues, the puzzle becomes even more complex. Each clue brings up a new puzzle to decipher. Solve all the puzzles and you can achieve your competitive advantage—marketing nirvana.

Identify Your Product

Divine how it fulfills your customers' needs. You should be able to predict your customers' reactions when they buy the service or product. Are consumers going to feel that this will make their lives somewhat better, and in what way?

Identify Your Positioning

The old newspaper rule for the lead sentence in an article is the 5 Ws and the H. They are the keys to a winning, relevant, emotional relationship with your customer, too.

▷ Who is the product for?
▷ What will the product do for the customer, psychologically and physically?
▷ Why would the consumer want it?

▷ When should the consumer use it?
▷ Where should the product be found?
▷ How is it going to affect the consumer's life, for the better?

Identify Your Target Consumers—and Their Expectations

The purpose of identifying your customers' lifestyle preferences is to build an ongoing relationship with them. You do this by identifying their expectations and the satisfactions they seek.

When a person finally commits to buying a product, he or she expects to receive certain performance cues. If there are no performance cues, consumers have no reason to buy the product again—even if it works.

Let's take a typical lightbulb, for example. Most consumers don't know how long a lightbulb lasts. They notice it only when it goes out. They may buy long-life bulbs and totally forget that they bought them. There are no performance cues. But if the shape of the bulb is changed, or perhaps the bulb dims for a brief second when the light is turned on, that becomes the cue that the product is indeed special.

Consumers buy end results, naturally. But determining what the end result of using your product actually is can be problematical. There can be a fine line between physical and emotional product benefits.

▷ Flavor may not be considered an emotion, but the anticipation of a positive sensory experience is. So is the satisfaction of having your thirst quenched in a new way.
▷ A scent is not an emotion, but the anticipation of a smell is. Two of the most remembered scents are Crayola crayons and Noxzema skin cream. They immediately recall childhood memories.

A scent may also be a reinforcement that a particular job has been done right. A residual bleach smell might reinforce to the person who washes clothes that the laundry is as clean as can be: "So clean I can actually smell it."
▷ Saving money is not an emotion, but saving money on a superior product shows consumers that they're smart.

▷ Anticipation of an event is an emotion. The major theme parks try to make sure people are waiting on lines at all the attractions. That is the performance cue. If visitors don't see a line, they think a ride is weak. If they don't see other people queued, they don't anticipate that the ride will be exciting. Anticipation of a trip or a wedding is usually more emotional than the actual experience. Watch for the next airline commercial. The planes are usually taking off, rather than landing. Travel is not an emotion, but wanderlust is. Part of the fun is thinking of getting there.

▷ A low-budget movie by a new filmmaker will often get better reviews from its audience than a film made once the filmmaker becomes much better known. The audience doesn't expect much the first time. The next time, the audience has higher expectations, and the film has to deliver.

In a business-to-business situation, particularly on a long-term project, the performance cue and expectation reinforcement is a demonstration of ongoing progress toward a goal. Don't wait six weeks before you show storyboards or whatever your assignment is. Constantly show the progress that is being made. Even simple memos can comfort your customers by showing that you are on top of things and thinking of them every waking moment.

Identify Your Customers' Mind-Set

Use psychology, not statistics. Someone, probably Mark Twain (he said everything else), said that there are three kinds of lies: lies, damned lies, and statistics. Customers are not statistics. They are you and your loved ones. They are the people next door.

Just as we train circus seals to jump through hoops of flames, we can do amazing things with numbers when we put our minds to it. Statistics are the junk food of marketers, especially those who are too insecure to sell their own critical judgments to management and need a prickly hedge to hide behind. They're aphrodisiacs to novice marketers who so much want their ideas to succeed that they ignore vital and obvious consumer signals.

Don't get caught in the "customers as digits" syndrome. Many marketers get excited about an idea through the sheer power of numbers. Typical of this is a business plan for a beverage or snack food that has to capture only 1 percent of a market to survive. That's right, the marketer shouts—"If only one out of every hundred people buys our product once a week, we'll have a $25 million business!" The trouble is, it doesn't work that way, even though it looks good on the premarket report or business plan. It doesn't work that way because your competitors are probably pitching the same product to the same consumers.

Numbers are often merely abstract information about the past. They are raw data for interpretation, more a reflection of the interpreter than of hard realities.

For instance, PepsiCo took an enormous financial blow when it introduced that fabulous fiscal failure Crystal Pepsi. The rationale for marketing what was to become a clear loser was explained this way: "We did intensive consumer testing and uncovered a group of consumers that wanted an alternative cola." Consumers are also against pollution and junk foods, but that doesn't mean that they are going to pay to get rid of either of them. It's more financially rewarding to watch people salivate at the idea of cookie dough ice cream than to read lists of numbers on an attribute table that show that on a scale of 1 to 100, people rate cookie dough a minus 20 in perceived healthfulness.

Identify the Distinguishing Characteristics of Your Product

These can be emotional or rational. They can be as simple as a logo. That's why Intel sees to it that the phrase "Intel inside" is plastered on computers that feature its chips. People may or may not know who Intel is, but it sounds impressive. The computer companies that put the Intel logo on the machine are telling consumers that what is on the inside is as foxy as what is on the outside.

Identify Your Leadership Position

Every company does something better than anyone else. At least it should make that claim. Make your product stand out by being number one in some aspect of your category that consumers care about. "My company is best at _____ (fill in the blank) because we do _____ (fill in the blank), and we prove it to our customers by _____ (fill in the blank)."

Louis Rich, a meatpacker, has a line of turkey cold cuts. The company was stagnating by positioning itself against other makers of cold cuts with a higher-quality image. But Louis Rich made a great turkey hot dog. It proclaimed a superior health positioning for its hot dogs over hot dogs in general. The positioning benefited the whole line.

Everybody likes to be number one. And most people like to buy from number one.

Identify Your Competitors and Know How They Will React

Entrepreneurial companies often create intriguing products for niche markets, then watch helplessly as the big guys steal them. That's because the conglomerates treat the niche markets as the minor leagues. They let the minors develop the product niche the way a minor-league team develops raw pitching talent. As soon as a product area becomes big enough to achieve major-league status, the big companies will take over, just as the major-league team spirits away the pitching talent the farm team has developed.

This doesn't have to happen. If you factor in the big guns when you develop the marketing plan, you can stay one step ahead of them with new enhancements to your product. Share of Heart is your advantage in the marketplace because big companies have trouble copycatting the special image the small entrepreneur has developed. Quaker's acquisition of Snapple brought high hopes but disappointing sales because Quaker couldn't transfer the Snapple founders' links to consumers. Frito-Lay bought Smartfood, but the product advertising lost its quirkiness when it was taken out of the hands of its founder.

You can buy a business.

You can be taught a business.

But it's hard to continue a brand personality that you didn't develop yourself. That's the small business advantage.

How motivated will the big companies be to spend against your marketing foray? It's imperative that you know, in general terms, how much your competitors will spend against you and what they will throw at you. Remember, pride has as much to do with your competitors' reaction as sheer dollar volume. When Arm & Hammer introduced its fabric softener, it knew that Lever Brothers would spend heavily on its competing Snuggle fabric softener. Lever Brothers would offer coupons and discounts in all areas where the Arm & Hammer product would be introduced. So Arm & Hammer introduced its own coupons and relied on the strong Arm & Hammer name to elicit repeat purchases.

Sommers successfully identified his competitors' strengths and weaknesses and those of his potential customers. Now, finally, some cigarette companies are developing their own boutique cigarettes, but American Spirit is the preemptive leader in this niche category.

Identify Cultural and Transcultural Opportunities

Salsa now outsells ketchup. Six new bagel stores opened in one town in New Mexico in one week. Taco Bell is synonymous with burritos—American style. (Taco Bell actually opened a very Mexican-looking facility in Mexico. Business was weak because it didn't look American enough for Mexicans.) All of these market trends are the result of the juxtaposition of the tiles in the cultural mosaic of America. For some strange reason, many people west of New York dislike New Yorkers. So Pace Salsa ran a commercial that said that the competition was from NEW YAAAWWWK City.

I don't know why these biases exist, but if you're a marketer, you should learn cultural anomalies and take advantage of them. Bueno Foods in New Mexico started as a small company freezing and preparing chili pepper for mainly Hispanic New Mexicans. When Tex-Mex food became big, it quickly expanded its product base with Hispanic prepared foods. Many fashion trends started by African-Americans slowly but surely filter down to a more mainstream Caucasian audience.

Identify the Economic Opportunity or Create One

Don't be afraid to reinvent the wheel. Bicycle manufacturers are constantly reinventing the wheel. And they're opening up untapped markets of people who *believe* these new wheels make them go faster or further.

Supermarketing: Taking Out the Fat

Entenmann's bakery successfully reinvented its whole product line for a new market that demanded reduced-fat desserts. Entenmann's made a good many of its cakes fat-free. Since this was long before "fat-reduced" line extensions became mandatory in almost all food categories, the company was taking a big chance. If Entenmann's was going to prepare low-fat products, it had to make sure that current customers looking for its traditional cakes wouldn't be turned off by the low-fat recipes. It also had to make sure it could technologically deliver a good-tasting fat-free product and that its retailers would continue to carry the product. The gutsy move worked. Entenmann's virtually reinvented the company overnight and preempted the fat-free baked goods category.

The Segment Key

Let's assume you have the next big idea. You've done your concept homework and identified the aspect of your product that best turns consumers on. You know what features your product should have and the necessary consumer performance cues to reinforce the benefits. From your consumers' perspective, your product is better than your competitors' products.

Now it's time to dig deep into your strongest consumer segment. Segmenting your market means concentrating your efforts where you have the strongest influence. Often, the largest segment is a mirage. It's the toughest to target efficiently because it tends to be amorphous. If you don't have a specific segmentation target, your money will be spent haphazardly.

Heartfelt Segmentation

Segmenting your market means that you have to make your emotional connections to various targetable groups of consumers. This is called *Heartfelt Segmentation*. It focuses on the primary emotional benefit consumers seek. Nordstrom's department stores use Heartfelt Segmentation to great success. The company pampers its customers and really makes shopping a pleasant experience. Compare this with Macy's, which makes shopping an adversarial procedure. Nordstrom's does well. Macy's is constantly in financial trouble even though its prices are usually lower than Nordstrom's. The triumph of heart over head again.

Many marketing people use a consumer's financial profile when they seek segmentation because these numbers jump off the page at you and there are numerous sources for them. But you can segment by consumer behavior and emotional benchmarks.

Emotional, lifestyle variables can be a key to dividing up a market because they get beneath surface attributes. They are more powerful than merely physical attributes.

You can use consumer groups to get at Heartfelt Segmentation possibilities. One of the common falsehoods about consumer groups is that the findings are not projectable. While the numbers can't be plotted on a computer, the emotional reactions certainly are projectible. If two people out of ten in your consumer groups are in love with your product, then you can have a success, provided you've elicited these responses in a number of groups across geographical boundaries.

At a consumer group study for a new dog food, one of the products shown was a dog food with a taste like "outdoor game" (the product was code-named Bambi Burgers—marketing people have warped senses of humor). Most of the people in the groups rejected the product vociferously. But in every group at least two consumers wanted the product badly. To judge the force of the reaction, the moderator spotlighted a particularly mousy consumer:

"Everyone here thinks you're really a terrible person for wanting this product," he said.

"But I would buy this product because my husband likes the taste of game," the respondent retorted.

"It's going to cost much more per bag than regular dog foods," said the moderator.

"I would buy it anyway," said the respondent, who was now being questioned like a defendant rather than a respondent.

Although the company eventually rejected the product because of the danger of negative publicity, it would have been a good segmentation strategy candidate, since in every group at least two people *strongly* wanted it.

Heartfelt Segmentation variables include not only age and financial worth but also such things as:

▷ Product loyalty
▷ Self-esteem
▷ Ambition
▷ Desire to change one's life habits (the midlife crisis is key to selling certain cars and motorcycles)
▷ Desire to love
▷ Desire to be loved
▷ Desire for social change

In fact, almost any of the hot buttons in Chapter 3 can lead to a market segmentation strategy. Any group of people is reachable, but not always through typical media plans. Sommers chose alternative magazines to target those consumers who see themselves as individuals and not part of the mainstream tobacco market.

Stark numbers can lead to insights that can lead to segmentation possibilities when you look beyond the black-and-white marketing printouts.

A certain direct mail marketer looks at numbers big-time and can find a business opportunity on a page full of digits. He does it in a different way from most marketers. He doesn't look for a particular item purchased, he looks for clues to an emotional involvement. For instance, if a consumer has a $500 investment in just about anything, that person is a strong potential customer—a passionately involved one—for a wide range of related products. For example, if you have made a $500 investment in cookbooks, you will probably be very receptive to offerings of new food products, cooking courses, or cooking implements.

The emotionally vested consumer seeks to enhance and protect his or her equity the same way a company might. Computer people are strong targets for software, computer magazines, and add-ons. A person with a collection of hand tools would be a major target for woodworking products and how-to magazines.

Special occasions are also distinct segmentation possibilities based on emotion. The consumer wants to buy something not only to please the person who is having a birthday, but the giver wants to look good through the totality of the gift package. We are not only "what we buy" but "what we give." American Express has been very successful with its prestigious American Express Gift Cheques. They take the crassness out of giving money. The distinctive wrapping downplays the money aspect and makes an elegant gift.

Following are some numbers and "paranoia checks" you can use to create a realistic decision tree and to decide whether a market segment is worth pursuing. They will do a lot to help you determine whether your market will be large enough—or whether you're better off having a few beers and forgetting the whole thing.

▷ *How big is the market for the product in dollar volume?* Is it really going to be worth your while? This can be tricky because you first have to determine what your market is. In the past several years marketers have fallen all over themselves pursuing the microwave market, only to find out that it is an illusion. This "market" is made up of segments instead of the one gigantic amorphous mass that looks so good on spreadsheets and in pre-market projections.

▷ *What market does your product belong to, from a behavioral and attitudinal standpoint?* Many food marketers get hung up on the presumed size of the "convenience food market." But it's incredibly small. The market is not for easy-to-prepare foods, but for tasty foods that consumers want that are also easy to prepare. For many consumers, a convenience food is one that can be purchased at a convenience store and eaten in a car.

▷ *Are you selling what's selling?* Is the market gaining or losing steam? I still find it funny when more and more companies jump on the bandwagon long after the show has left town. In many industries—wood stoves and pellet stoves, midrange computers, high-tech sound systems—the years of supergrowth are over. When business is good, few people have to look at the bottom line. When business is bad, people have to work harder because the bottom feeders are preying. Bottom feeders are those consumers who are "waiting for the price to come down." But these people are not just looking for lower prices, they're looking for "supercharged" products at lower prices. By constantly updating your products, you can help your customer "keep down with the Joneses."

▷ *Where are the sales going to come from?* Into which pocket is the consumer going to reach to pay for your product? Is it brought with discretionary money, family food money, impulse money? Discretionary money is usually the first to go in a recession.

The Focus Key

It's nice to be a general practitioner, but a specialist makes more money. Plus, you get all those fancy machines that look so impressive to the patient. A specialist uses all those machines to focus his or her resources on a single proposition.

Consider yourself a specialist using all available resources to diagnose a consumer problem and act on it in a concentrated way. Use constant vigilance to keep in touch with what your customers want and then give it to them faster and add more substance than anyone else.

Once again, it's important to know your assets so that you know what to focus on. The Slim-Fast company was known for its diet product: Ultra Slim-Fast Shakes. Its slogan was almost as well known as its product: "A shake for breakfast, a shake for lunch and a sensible dinner." Then the company lost its way—and its focus. It rushed headlong into an ill-conceived expansion. It branched out into dinner entrées, snack foods, and a whole group of juice products that diluted its basic premise. Slim-Fast's president, Danny Abraham, thought that consumers were buying the company's products for health reasons, whereas they were really buying them as diet aids. Slim-Fast parlayed its enormous consumer leverage into big losses. In short, it diverted itself from its customer-oriented Share of Heart and lost its main emotional connection with consumers.

Find your niche and grow with it. Focus and build your brand's emotional value. Focusing is similar to segmentation because you must define and build on what you do best. And once again you have to go back to your mission statement and ask, "What business am I in? What business should I be in?" It can be a major mistake to go beyond your sphere of influence, as Slim-Fast did, even if a market appears to exist.

Focusing is a state of mind. While many companies focus on building profits—and for sure that is the ultimate goal—growth companies focus on satisfying markets and building on their basic consumer-driven premises.

Life used to be simple. You could cook up a fairly useful product, advertise it on TV, and be sure of a certain market share. It's become a lot more complicated. Take the air freshener category. It used to be enough to put some fragrance in an aerosol can and spray a new scent. Now there are deodorants for every room in the house. There are products for drawers, the kitchen, and the living room. There are products that mask specific odors, such as mildew and cat-box odor. And of course there are potpourri packets, candles, and electrical gadgets—Plug-Ins. All of these products are sold on the emotion, or hot button, of security. People want to feel secure about their homes when guests visit. Indeed, the user's nose becomes accustomed to scents rather quickly and really can't smell the delivered fragrance for more than a few seconds. In the freshener category, Glade, by concentrating on adding scents for specific customer-perceived needs, has beaten its archcompetitor Airwick. Airwick is owned by Reckitt & Colman, which has many divisions and major problems with focusing on their specific product lines.

A bit player or small marketing department can have an advantage over the big guns in a particular category because the smaller player can react faster without being overwhelmed by the need to compile lists of numbers for each new round of management approvals. It can focus on emotions and consumer-driven benefits because it can see the reactions firsthand without reading through research reports.

A sharply segmented market is the easiest to focus on. The harder you have to reach for your customers, the less efficient your marketing program is going to be. A sales projection chart that shows that sales are spread out around the country is dangerously misleading. The more scattered your sales are, the more complex and expensive it's going to be to reach that market. This has been a major problem with the marketing of "health foods." Before the arrival of the health food superstore, the health food business, traditionally mom-and-pop operations, couldn't generate enough concentrated volume to provide a healthy financial return. Marketing through these outlets may be great for the soul, but it's lousy for the pocketbook.

Those with a less focused approach, who try to be everything to everybody, end up pleasing no one. When you decide on your customer fit and work toward satisfying that fit, your marketing plan will be more profitable and effective.

The Attack Key

Here's the fun part. Everything else was just planning. Now you get to attack, using all the knowledge you've compiled. There are many books on how to attack your market. If the book was written by an advertising person, it will tell you to spend bucks on advertising. Books on packaging and promotion will tell you to spend in those areas. But the real way to attack is to use all of the marketing disciplines. While a totally comprehensive attack plan is beyond the scope of this book, I can offer some tips.

The key words are *adapt* and *adopt*. Adapt your ideas, technologies, and resources to consumer needs that are ever-changing. Adopt the most promising positionings to deliver these needs.

Smart marketers know that instead of making consumers change their behavior and spending patterns to adapt to a product, the marketer must adapt to the way the customers think. Your customers often include distributors and retailers. They all require an emotional tithe.

The attack is where you assert your leadership position. Attack on all fronts. Promotion, advertising, and packaging should all feature a one-sentence unified theme that plays to the emotions. Slim-Fast's original strategy was genius in its simplicity.

You've Been Attacking All Along

While you've been compiling all the information in your planning stages, you've also been compiling ammunition for your attack.

▷ If you've identified your customers' mind-set, you can create ads and packaging that speak to your customers personally.

▷ If you've identified your leadership position, you can plaster it on all your sales materials and broadcast it to your distributors.

▷ If you've identified your competitors, you can one-up them in every aspect of your marketing thrust.

▷ If you've segmented your audience, you can choose the right outlets for your product.

▷ If you've identified the economic opportunity and can make good on it, you'll get placement in your market.

▷ If your attack is focused, you'll do it efficiently and quickly.

Courting the People Who Ultimately Sell Your Products

Unless you're selling directly to the consumer, your first contact is probably the retailer who sells your product or the distributor who sells the product to the retailer. These people are flooded with products. And retailers can be hard to work with. They have a major problem: They don't want to think. They don't want to bust their behinds selling your product, even if you've paid them large slotting allowances. They are just as happy renting shelf space as they are selling goods. When they put your product in the store, they want it to walk off the shelves. These people usually have one thing in mind: to make money as quickly as possible.

But your distributors and retailers are as vulnerable to an emotional pitch as your customer is. They get excited by knowing that they can draw new customers and increase their business incrementally. They can actually get worked up when you can prove to them that you know your market thoroughly and have drummed up consumer interest without their having to offer coupons.

Smartfood presold its product and created excitement through a grassroots campaign. Because the company was low on cash, it had to be creative in its marketing approach. In one advertising and public relations coup, it had people patrol beaches dressed like giant popcorn bags. Smartfood built up so much excitement that retailers were forced to carry the product by the strength of consumer demand.

As a rule, most retailers are very stiff-necked in their ways of doing business. They like to do things the way they've been doing them for years. Sometimes they're right, sometimes they're wrong, but it's their show, so you have to adapt your plan to fit in. They are also not very creative and will add little but a selling venue to your sales plan.

The product that obviously enhances the value of their stores and draws new customers will win out.

Retailers find security when you create an entire program instead of selling a single item or two. It's your job to make your sales program run on autopilot—and fulfill what you promise. Generate new enhancements to your product, new additions to your product line, or new advertising and promotions to keep pace with your retailers' expectations. This makes everyone happy.

Retailers stock it, ignore it (which usually happens), but collect their money. This is the way they like it. Retailers were not overwhelmed by the prospects of selling American Spirit cigarettes. It was the enthusiasm of Robin Sommers that pulled them in—and it was his knowledge of his market that made the product leap off the shelf with the same speed it went in.

Cross-Marketing Your Share of Heart

Cross-marketing is one of the hottest ways to make an impression on your distributors and your ultimate customers. Essentially, cross-marketing works as follows: You pair your products with other products in a store. In effect, you're selling the store's merchandise along with your own by enhancing the store's merchandise. Store owners are delighted, because you're actually increasing sales of the store's other merchandise, and the store is turning a profit on your product too. Very few stores can turn this down.

A California games manufacturer set out to market a new game based on romance. After failing to impress merchants in traditional channels, he came up with the idea of cross-marketing his game in other kinds of stores. He chose merchants and companies that would have some kind of emotional affinity with his products. If there was none, he created one. He sold stores on the benefits of the entire sales program, which benefited everyone.

They included lingerie shops, hotels, lotions-and-potions shops, and even marriage counselors.

His first foray was a local lingerie store. The owners loved the program. The game helped romanticize the store window and decor, and helped the owners sell more lingerie. He sold the product to a lotions-and-potions store, and the store not only sold the game, but more fragrances and body gels. The Hyatt Hotel at Union Square in San Francisco saw the product and built a romantic promotion around it to get couples in the hotel during the normally slow weekend. Clergy and marriage counselors heard about the product from the parishioners, and ordered the game. Word of mouth kept spreading. Calls for the game flooded in. It was the totality of the product coupled with the up-front research that evolved into the marketing plan that made the product effective and set the stage for new products.

Advancing the Seller's Equities

If you're selling into a department store, you should make it as easy as possible for your product to sell itself without the aid of a salesperson.

If you have a product that you would like to get on the major shopping networks, your attack plan should be to show how easy the product is to demonstrate. Your research into your TV markets should clearly demonstrate how well your product fits into their audience profiles.

The Evolve Key

Ted Williams used to say that hitting a baseball is the toughest activity in sports. The batter has a three-inch-wide wooden stick in his hand and is trying to pummel a sphere that's coming right at him, and maybe curving, even at ninety miles an hour.

Like a batter, you must move with the speed of a thrown ball, constantly evolving your product and your marketing strategy, and, like the pitcher, you must always give your competitors new curves to follow. Your changes should be planned at least six months in advance, always relying on new research and on evolving consumer needs.

Bankers and investors love this advance planning. A venture capitalist sat in rapt attention as the representative of a prospective venture company unfolded her plans to him. Not only did she have a bright new product, she had developed a series of contingency plans that were to go into effect as soon as competition entered the market. Her plans included product changes, new promotions, and ongoing research into new markets.

The venture guy backed the business.

Lay the Groundwork to Compete

While no one can guarantee the success of any marketing venture, there are steps that can be taken to eliminate much of the guesswork. With the proper groundwork, the smaller entrepreneur can compete against the marketing dynamos when these steps are followed systematically, but creatively. All products flow from the ultimate buyer.

▶ 6

Creating Share of Heart From the Start: Developing New Product Winners

In the 1990s Nestlé and Pepsi created a joint venture to mass-market iced coffee in supermarkets and other mass markets. The rationale was as follows: Iced coffee was a huge market in Japan and iced tea was a big winner in the United States. Thus (the premise continued algebraically), iced coffee should be a hit. The venture failed.

The reason: Iced tea can be guzzled. Iced coffee is sipped. Americans want their pleasures fast. They want to guzzle.

Aseptic packaging (those little shelf-stable boxes) has not captured as big a market in the United States as it has in Europe.

The reason: We had refrigerators long before Europeans did. A shelf-stable product is not perceived as fresh. That's why shelf-stable retort packaging for dinner entrées has never made it big-time.

By all rights, new product development shouldn't be too hard. Companies have been introducing new products as long as there have been companies. So why do the vast majority of new products fail? If you ask marketers, they will put the blame on:

1. Declining brand loyalty
2. The current economic climate
3. The failure of the planets and stars to align properly

These aren't the real reasons. The three real reasons are:

1. Products are built on the wrong consumer premises.
2. Products have too few distinguishing characteristics.
3. There is not enough up-front probing into consumer motivations.

The last is the key reason new products fail—and such probing is the best way to prevent the others.

The failure rate is not going to change in the near future, because marketers place little importance on probing into the irrational human heart—except after the product is produced. And even then, it's usually just in the ads. By then it's too late: The product has been built.

The smarter way is to determine what consumers want to buy and make it for them, instead of making something and trying to convince consumers with advertising that they want it. It's easier. Almost painless. Your mantra should be:

Find out what consumers want—and the way they want it.
Find out the way they want it sold to them.
Sell it to them that way.

Part of the problem is that marketers are uncomfortable with anything they can't plot on a graph. In the traditional failure-ridden new product development program, R&D, marketing, or some misguided, overextended entrepreneur comes up with an alleged breakthrough idea. The developer hopes and prays that he or she can sell it to someone. Whether someone wants or needs the product is of small concern, because our manager or entrepreneur is too wrapped up in the details of making the thing or too busy putting together long lists of unrelated numbers to back up his or her own preconceived notions.

Most companies continue to develop products that they want to sell, rather than what consumers want to buy. This is especially sad in the case of the smaller entrepreneur who spends his or her life savings developing and attempting to market a product, and hoping it would be successful, when he or she had spent more on up-front groundwork and research into consumer sensitivities.

In larger companies, the opposite occurs. Hundreds of thousands of dollars are spent on misguided research that tells you everything about consumers except the one key factor: what product they want to buy, given half a chance.

Why is it that product development people will spend zillions of dollars on molds and complicated prototypes, yet grow apoplectic when asked to divert a few of those dollars toward research into the warm fuzzies that can drive their market?

It's even more ridiculous that managers will spend up to $100,000 on video presentations to sell the idea to their own management.

Here's the usual new product development and design procedure. A group of people assemble in a room with computers, notepads, blueprints, and a trusty overhead projector. Some of them show their ideas to the others, who say, "That's a great idea." Then they offer one another congratulations. It's like a "Marriage Encounter" with lab coats (or suits and ties).

Then, they take their trusty overhead projector and add a VCR. They pitch their concepts to management. Columns of digits jump magically through the air. The video shows the great lengths the designer went to to make the product. Management makes "improvements" and congratulates the designers on their wonderful work. Then the suppliers are brought in from the outside to make the product a reality.

Finally, when the product hits Joe's Pushcart Joblot three-for-a-dollar aisles, everyone laments, "Wasn't that a great idea? Too bad it was ahead of its time."

And here's what they say to the media (I actually read this three times in six months from three unrelated companies): "The initial excitement was short-lived. Our research shows that consumers like it, but the frequency wasn't there. Basically we didn't sell enough to make it work."

But guys, why didn't you realize that in the first place?

Why doesn't anyone bother to ask the people who are expected to purchase the product for opinions before spending the big bucks? It's not enough to launch a good product into the market-

place today. You need a great product, one that is truly meaningful to customers. If your product is so-so, you might as well stay
home and play poker with the boys. And you have to make sure
you have an audience that will genuinely want your product.

Dealing with consumers and learning what emotions drive
the category, particularly in the early stages of product development, is your head start on the competition. You're going to need
this head start, because if your product is a success, it's going to
be knocked off by the competition a maximum of six months
later. Consumers should be brought into the new product
process and questioned at the very beginning.

Entering a new market with a new product can be daunting.
The path to a successful new product is rarely linear because you're
venturing on an uncharted path. Like a rugged mountain path, it is
full of twists, sharp turns, bumps, and potential roadblocks.

But you can go up the mountain safely and surely if you
pave the way with consumer insights. The trick is to expose your
products and positionings to consumers at all stages to make
sure you're getting it right.

You can even adapt your competitors' products to your own
fiscal and marketing needs. It's easier to steal market share from
a competitor than to blaze a new marketing path, especially if
you know that the insights that spawned the market are genuine.
Barbara's Bakery, a natural foods manufacturer, has a simple
recipe for success. It specializes in creating innovations by taking
an idea that has been successful in the mass market and making
it all-natural for sales in health food stores. Ironically, the company is now getting placement in mainstream supermarkets.

The Strength of the Word *New*

New is one of the strongest words in the English language (*free* is
the strongest). Consumers want to try your new product. They
want to recommend your new product to their friends and associates. It's très chic to be the first on your block to discover a new
product, just as it boosts your self-esteem to be the first one to try
a new four-star restaurant.

Yes, consumers are engulfed in an avalanche of new products—mostly parity products or those that marketing mavens

deprecate as low-interest products. But, just as a bird surrounded by a forest of trees will pick out the tiniest twig that fits its needs, the consumer will focus on the product that speaks to her or his feelings. Like the bird, the consumer screens out the irrelevant and focuses on the relevant.

But marketers often forget this, and instead create products and product differentiations that have absolutely no relevance to consumers. On the drawing board they may look exciting, but even the most common-sense products will often flub the "will consumers buy it" test, as follows:

Several companies have tried to market little stickers that are placed on food packages in the refrigerator. When the product has been stored too long (say a week), the sticker changes color. That sounds great—now you'll know how long those leftovers have been sitting around. The problem is, the caretaker of the household really doesn't want to know that the food has been just sitting there. He or she thinks, "It's still edible," and it may well be. If the person sees that a sticker has changed color, he or she feels like a poor homemaker. Consumers *would* like to see these stickers on products in the store. The trouble is, the supermarkets don't want their customers to know how long their products have been sitting around.

Wesson Oil came up with a new cooking spray that shouted, "no alcohol." Who cared? Not consumers. They didn't even know that spray-on oils contained alcohol.

Companies fell all over themselves to develop an "Internet only" computer marketed to consumers. Why would anyone want a dedicated Internet machine when, for a few hundred dollars more, he or she could buy a computer that entertains and educates?

Consumers and marketers have different sets of values. Where the marketer is concerned with what little gizmo she or he can put into the product to get a competitive edge, the customer is saying, "I don't care about your competitive edge. What's in it for me?"

Here's an example.

General Electric learned how to squeeze more usable light out of its lightbulbs.

It initially marketed these Miser lights on the proposition of saving 5 watts of electricity out of each 100-watt bulb. This ignored the fact that few consumers read their electric bills and even fewer know what a watt actually is. Thus, consumers were vitally uninterested. Although GE had this "can't miss" technology, consumers couldn't relate the benefits to their own lives. Since the energy savings were a minuscule portion of the utility bill, there was no visual cue and no value reinforcement.

GE then changed the positioning, which fixed the product. It positioned the bulb to give consumers a bonus of extra wattage: 100 watts of power out of a 90-watt bulb. More light for your money—that's a benefit. That's a service that almost any consumer can relate to. It's especially important to baby boomers as they get grayer and grayer. As they get older, they need more light to read by. The benefit reinforces itself every time the user turns on the light. No need to call the kids to read the fine print.

Learn Passions and Perceptions Before You Produce

A successful effort doesn't begin with a product, it begins with positioning research that identifies an underlying consumer need—even a passion. New product work is most successful when you don't try to outguess consumers. Consumers are always ahead of the manufacturer because they have all the leverage. It's called a checkbook. They use it when they're finally convinced the purchase is right. Finding the optimum hook is the single most important aspect of creative marketing; it is as important as the big product idea. The hook should be more than an aspect or feature of the product. The hook is the totality of the product experience.

Although take-out food should taste the same as the identical food from the same restaurant, it never does. Those take-out foam containers seem to deaden the taste of the finest food. Furthermore, the decor of the restaurant and the attentiveness of the waiters are nullified by the container. It's the totality of the dining experience that makes a restaurant worthwhile.

Don't spend tons of money developing your product in full without knowing the whole consumer-driven product story. Although it's hard not to, you can't fall in love with your product just because it's your baby. It's too expensive. Make sure consumers tell you it's a product they will buy and continue to buy.

Needs Waiting to Be Satisfied Are Everywhere

Needs can be self-gratifying, like a self-reward of a rich dessert or buying a piece of jewelry to pamper oneself. "When the going gets tough, the tough go shopping."

Needs can be of the nurturing variety: the desire to treat a family or child to the best care imaginable.

People are sensual beings. They have a need for stimulation. Even something as banal as dishwashing detergent can be sensual when we add a "great lemon scent." Microwave popcorn is sensual as tempting aromas are wafted through the house. The world was very happy with a computer that merely beeped. But computer users became downright ecstatic when the Soundblaster created lifelike sounds that took users away from their real-world problems. On the negative side, Free & Soft was a fabric softening packet that was meant to be stuck on the inside of a clothes dryer. It was a flop as a product because it couldn't be smelled. Even though lab tests showed that Free & Soft delivered as much softening power as more-expensive-per-wash dryer sheets, the product offered no sensory reward to consumers.

The Critical Path to Success

You owe it to yourself and to your company not to let guesswork get in the way. Let the energy of the consumer's emotions drive the product from its inception. Don't entrust the product's positioning to an advertising agency that has nothing to do with its development.

This path is a proactive approach to new product development. It's an expansion of the program shown in Chapter 2. It will show you whether your product is truly different, and if it is, it will show you whether the difference is important enough to consumers to make them buy it. You'll learn how to position your product or product differentiation so that it is truly meaningful to consumers. Just as important, it will show you what is not effective.

According to your resources and goals, hypothesize products and benefits that you can produce. At the same time, guess at needs that can be satisfied by the product. Probe for consumer reaction by showing consumers real-world advertising featuring the product and the putative consumer benefit. Keep working on your product's positioning until the ideas have evolved to a point where a solid group of consumers want the product and you know the hot buttons that make them want it.

In short, create hypothetical products, and put them in a real-world setting. When consumers say, "Yes, I'd buy that product," you know you have a winner.

There are great advantages to developing a new product based on consumer feedback rather than from the confines of your office or kitchen.

▷ New product opportunities and purchase triggers are developed simultaneously. You can cut your losses by quitting on a bad idea early if you can't find a way to sell your dream clearly and effectively.

▷ Physical product benefits and the consumer perception of physical and emotional benefits are defined, so that you know what bells and whistles you should incorporate into your product. A short time ago a high-tech shopping cart was introduced to supermarkets. The carts featured a computerized product locator and a calculator. The carts were removed after a test market stint because of lack of consumer interest. As one consumer wrote in a letters to the editor column, "I was upset that all the pretty shopping carts that matched my car were gone." The maker of these carts filed for Chapter 11 bankruptcy. This wouldn't have happened if the company had checked the product for consumer reaction first.

▷ New product opportunities are defined in terms of your equity and resources. These opportunities can be a famous brand name, a special distribution channel, a technological breakthrough, or even just a desire to break into an area. Here's a story of defining one's asset and building on it.

Kinko's is a chain of twenty-four-hour copy shops that bills itself as "Your office on the road." Kinko's started as a coffee shop in a college town. It had a copy machine in the back and ran copies twenty-four-hours a day. The owner, Paul Orfalia, was no dummy. He knew that his prime asset was the all-hours copier that was prized by every procrastinating student. So he slowly built a chain of copy centers in college towns and gave the coffee away free!

Faux Ads

After you have the product idea, work the product out on paper in the form of faux ads. The use of these ads was discussed in the context of marketing in general in Chapter 3. Let's go into a bit more detail about why these ads are so important and how we use consumers.

Why ads? Developing ads before you make your product forces you to look at your product from a marketing standpoint. If you can't sell the product or service with an ad that focuses on a single selling proposition, the chances are you won't be able to sell it at all. When you sell your product, you're going to have to communicate your product to someone. Doesn't it make sense to get a head start on the process?

Why ads? Because paper is a hell of a lot cheaper than prototypes. Ads allow you to experiment on paper every step of the way and validate every part of your product before you physically make it. This will help you find fatal flaws faster. It's cheaper to build a house when you know what the occupants want and you don't have to guess at what they may want. You can create twenty or so full-color concepts with a unlimited variation of ideas for a fraction of the cost of one product prototype.

Why ads? Because you can keep the creative envelope stretching until it snaps. The nice thing about doing the preliminary work with ads and instant consumer feedback is that you don't have to be afraid to make mistakes. You can explore every creative whim. Ads also allow you to make modifications to your product before it goes into the real world.

People often ask, "How can you develop an ad for a product that doesn't exist?" Why not? The people who write the ads and produce the tantalizing trailers for movies do it all the time.

The ads, TV commercials, and trailers are finished well before the movie is produced.

Most major movies are pretested too. If the ending doesn't play well, the producers can change it. If the characters don't play well, they can be fleshed out in the editing room. Imagine how bad Kevin Costner's box office flop *Waterworld would* have been if it had not been fixed up after consumer testing.

Build Your Product for Consumers

Show these ads to groups of consumers who represent what you think is your target market. The key is to get consumers to react, because in the real world consumers react to everything they see. Consumers don't try to become marketing experts and analyze why they should buy a product. They simply buy or don't buy.

Obviously you can't show your product to millions of people. And even if you could, there are thousands of products out there, so you must show consumers why your product is special. That's why you seek out anything that will arouse fervor in consumers. You show your ads and positionings to consumers through interactive groups, as discussed in Chapter 3.

But don't rely entirely on interactive groups and an outside moderator. Talk to consumers one on one. You, and everyone connected in any way with new product development, should question consumers too. A relatively painless way is to have a mall facility intercept consumers for you. Then use your boards to gauge consumer reaction.

When you show your ads to consumers, several things can happen.

▷ They may like the product but hate the positioning. You're alive.
▷ They may like the positioning but hate the product. You're alive.
▷ Or they may give you the dreaded "I'd buy it if I had a coupon" response—which means they won't buy your product. You're dead.

Usually, you'll find that 90 percent of your ideas will be shot down for various reasons. Isn't it funny? That's about the same rate as new product failures. The focus group will become your adversary. But fear not. You haven't squandered much money or resources. Remember, this is just paper. The consumer group is not your enemy, it is your safety net.

Building on Rejections

Rejection is a vital part of the new product process. In fact, rejection is to be encouraged. If you don't get rejections, you're simply not working hard enough or expanding the creative envelope. You're being held captive to your own judgment and preconceived ideas, and you're going to pay at test market time. Count on your favorite ads and products dying a horrible death until you learn more about and gain insights into the specific market.

If you don't build on rejection, you're also apt to throw away a good idea. Building on rejection is the optimum way to refine your product and, just as important, your consumer sales pitch. Consumer groups act as your idea "refinery," sifting through the slag and leaving you with the gold.

I was part of the team that helped create the hugely successful Glad-Lock bags (the yellow-and-blue seal becomes green). After the first two interactive groups, the outlook was bleak. Consumers thought they were being taken for dolts. This is not a good way to build a loyal market. Almost every woman—we used women because we guessed they would be the ultimate purchasers—vituperatively rejected the product.

So we went back and licked our wounds. We remembered hearing one woman say that she thought the product was ridiculous, but she wished she could find a way to get her husband and kids to wrap up foods. We came back with the following positioning: "The bag that's so simple, even husbands and kids get it right every time." To consumers, the product was no longer ridiculous. It was truly meaningful. The new positioning, which allowed consumers to rationalize the color-change seal, struck an immediate chord with them. Just this minor change in positioning overcame the years of lead time enjoyed by Dow's Ziploc.

The point is, if we hadn't been rejected, we would not have developed the strategy that worked so well. Even today, commercials take extra care to make sure the housewife is not insulted by the pitch.

Every rejection should lead to an insight, and therefore an improvement in your product or positioning. Remember, if you polarize people with your new product idea, at least you know that you know one segment will strongly want your product.

A strong no is much better than a weak yes. Good restaurateurs will tell you that the worst kind of customer is one who dines agreeably, leaves, and never returns. The progressive restaurateur builds from what the dissatisfied customers say (as well as the regular customers) and fixes what's wrong.

Actively solicit rejection. Try asking consumers to write the product's obituary at the end of the groups. What they will tell you can be extraordinarily helpful because it will underscore what's bad about your product so that you can fix it.

Negative insights can be a hidden road map to a new idea. Staying flexible and making adjustments is key.

Honing in on Sensory Appeals in a Consumer-Oriented Manner

It's important that your product appeal to as many senses as possible, but your sensory benefits should not stand alone, as in a blind taste test or aroma test. Consumers put sensory attributes into their own frame of reference. Sensory appeal is one of the aspects of your product, but don't stop at a smell or taste that's good. Test the whole concept. Smells have traditionally been a difficult area for market testers. Usually consumers are given a vial of something to smell and asked their opinions about it. In this situation, consumers can't give a helpful opinion because the smell is out of context. But if you demonstrate the appeal on a board or through imagery, consumers can better relate. For instance, if a consumer is given a vial of lavender to smell, a connection to the real world is hard to make. But if you say your new spray starch has a lavender scent and you use appealing graphics of a potpourri packet in an ad, the consumer will relate instantly. Than you can give her or him the vial and see if the aroma lives up to expectations.

Back to the Drawing Board

After the first round of groups, it's time to regroup. But now you have an incredible amount of learning. So you take your ads one by one and study them. What works you leave alone. What doesn't work you either throw out or improve.

You can change:

▷ Your product
▷ Your positioning
▷ Your to-the-heart selling premise

After each wave of groups (and between individual groups, if necessary), the concept inventory is totally modified. You can:

▷ Add new concepts.
▷ Drop concepts that didn't work at all.
▷ Modify concepts that seemed to have merit.
▷ Keep the strongest concepts. These will serve as benchmarks for your next set of groups.

Then you take your revised concepts out to new territories—wherever you think your target market is. If your product is national in scope, take it out to geographically diverse areas so that you get a representative sampling of the United States. If your product is regional, go to those areas that represent your target market. This is continued until:

▷ Synthesis of the most promising products *that you can act on* is realized.
▷ Positionings are defined.
▷ Purchase motivations are determined.

At the conclusion of the groups, the concepts will have gone through a comprehensive set of tests to confirm their validity, their communications value, and their impact. You will have developed strong, winning, advertisable product concept(s) that can be readily implemented. Your winning products and strategies will have struck a "targetable nerve." Moreover, these concepts were developed from expressed consumer needs and tested to make sure these needs were met by your product and positioning. (See Figure 6-1.)

Neither consumers nor the client were motivated by the positioning or the product shown in Figure 6-1A. Consumers *did* gravitate toward the "options" concept shown in Figure 6-1B, but reacted poorly to the negative treatment of other available fuels. From here, the idea evolved into a motivating concept (Figure 6-1C), which guided product prototypes and all communications.

What Is the Best Price?

Fortunately, you can also find out what your price should be in your focus group research. Just attach price bullets to your boards and see how they affect purchase interest. Try a number of prices until you find the one that fits best. Don't ask consumers what they would pay for the product. They will invariably say something incredibly low. Make them react—as they do in the real world.

Marketing Versus R&D: Winning the Battle

In one corner, weighing in with a curriculum vitae, wearing a lab coat and expressing a total distaste for marketing, is R&D.

In the other corner, weighing in with a simple résumé and dressed in a power suit and tie, is marketing.

There are no time limits. It is (seemingly) a no-holds-barred fight to the death.

The battle between marketing and R&D occurs because R&D people are often not considered part of the marketing team and therefore are not included in new product ventures. Or they're forced to react to half-baked mandates from marketing groups who put together a matched set of numbers and expect R&D to pull a product from the desk drawer. Like marketing, R&D is very defensive about any new product idea that doesn't come from the R&D team.

The role of R&D is often miscast by too many companies as the strategy of hope: Throw money in and hope R&D results.

(text continues on page 118)

Figure 6-1. The evolution of a concept from probable loser to winner.

A. Poor

(continues)

Figure 6-1. *(continued)*

B. Better

Don't "attack" wood or gas say "alternative"

If you thought your fireplace options were limited by the hassles of gas or wood, think again.

Name still not right

Introducing
GlowMaster
clean-burning fireplace insert

🔥 **Lights in seconds**
🔥 **Extinguishes in seconds**
🔥 **No smoke or pollutants**
🔥 **No ashes or residue.**
🔥 **Fully portable.**
🔥 **No installation!**

FREE!
Your first supply of Gel-Fuel for hours and hours of smokeless, pollutant free fireplace fires.

C. Best

The Common-Sense Alternative to Gas and Wood.

Introducing the all-new GelFuel™ insert!

A **GelFuel** fire is clean-burning, safe to the environment, quick and easy to light.

If you thought your fireplace options were limited to gas and wood, here's the alternative. The Gel Fuel fireplace insert.

It turns on in seconds with the touch of a match.

And it extinguishes in seconds at the touch of a lever.

It runs on a new kind of fuel that's totally smokeless. It's so clean, you can load it in your business suit.

It's so friendly to the environment you can even run it on no-burn days.

And best yet, nobody will know it's not a wood fire if you don't tell them.

And if you want your wood fire -- no problem. The Gel-fuel insert is so light-weight, it lifts right out of your fireplace.

The Gel Fuel fireplace insert. It's a new kind of energy you can live with.

The Common-Sense Alternative to Gas and Wood.

1660 E. Central Ave.   Seattle, WA. 09876
TOLL-FREE: 800-678-4563   FAX: 317-345-9821
Dealer Inquiries Invited.

Both marketing and R&D must know what the other's problems and challenges are. And they should constantly test each other to make sure everyone is pushing to the max and getting the most out of business opportunity. You should build relationships with R&D.

This happens by working in an intersecting plane with R&D instead of in parallel worlds. In theory, both groups share the same goals. R&D departments can be a great source of inspiration and even research and development, when they're worked with as key players rather than "those you have to deal with."

Great R&D advances rarely work in a vacuum. The marketing manager's goal is to provide a conduit and direction for new ideas. An effective management trick is to design a product idea that is just beyond R&D's current reach. Make it a personal challenge: Challenge R&D to make the technologically unfeasible feasible. It's easier to pull back on your product demands than to add to them later. Our space program was a direct result of the concept of "innovating by necessity."

Look at it this way: If the product succeeds, everybody will take credit for it. If it fails, you can always blame R&D.

Recognizing a Winner

The president of a successful ceramics company said it best. "When I develop a new piece, I show it to my potential customers. If they smile when they see it, I know I have a winner."

▶ 7

Exploding Those Deadly Marketing Myths

The day is impossibly sunny—a perfect beach day for the family and kids. The ocean water, in one's imagination, is cool and turquoise and extends its personal invitation. Along ambles a playful little girl with a golden tan, romping on the beach, eating a dripping ice cream cone. She looks as if she wandered out of a Norman Rockwell painting. A pint-sized dog yips behind her. (Have you figured out the marketing scenario behind this picture yet?) The dog takes a playful nip at her bathing suit. A bit of pale flesh is exposed. (Now I know you've figured it out.)

It sounds like a corny opening of a third-rate kid's book, but it was that ad with a little child's bare butt that gave rise to Coppertone. After thirty years, and some minor updating here and there, the ad is as strong as it ever was. And the brand, with constant updating, is as strong as it ever was.

In marketing, nothing is for sure, except that you have to keep your résumé on hand and always updated. But there are three beliefs that are almost universally held by retailers and manufacturers alike. Although they are treated as if they were carved on stone tablets in MBA programs, these bromides are wrong. The good news is that these misconceptions mean big opportunities for creative marketers and MBAs who have seen the light. These beliefs are:

1. The (myth of) the product life cycle

2. The (myth of) the parity product
3. The (myth of) declining brand loyalty

These are just a few examples of self-fulfilling prophecies that hinder long-term product success.

Even though you have to memorize these maxims to graduate with an MBA, they are not facts of life. They're cute little catchphrases that seem to pop up more and more as people look for alibis for declining market share and diminishing product creativity. They're excuses—heresies against any marketing that requires thinking. Excuses for letting the bottom fall out of sales because the marketer was just too lazy or too scared of bucking accepted wisdom to do anything about it. These myths are self-fulfilling prophecies that are widespread simply because marketers have taken the heart, and thus the primary sales hook, out of the products and services they sell.

The Myth of the Product Life Cycle

In this insidious myth, a product lives, matures, and dies, like a living entity. This may work for frogs and butterflies, but it doesn't work for products, for they are provided for *by* a living, breathing entity: the brand manager or entrepreneur. If the life cycle exists, how do we account for products like Campbell's soups, Swift bacon, and Colgate toothpaste being among the market leaders for fifty—count 'em, fifty—years? Actually, Colgate-Palmolive had let Colgate toothpaste slip to a distant second to Crest in the oral care category before it decided to right itself and narrow the leadership gap with on-target line extensions a few years ago.

While the length of an organic life form's existence is finite, we can make brand and product lives infinite by playing mad Doctor Frankenstein and injecting new life into them once in a while. It's time to go out and rebuild your brands instead of throwing them onto the scrap heap!

Marketers give up on their brands long before consumers do. The reason they give up on them is insensitivity:

▷ To their company
▷ To their brand's emotional pull
▷ To consumer concerns

Brand managers get bored with a product long before consumers do. Or marketing ranks are replenished by new cohorts of managers who don't have the same emotional commitment to the product as the original creator. The first brand manager loves the product, brings it to life, nurtures it, treats it as his or her baby. The next manager treats it as an adopted child, the third as a bastard, orphaned waif. It's the Peter Principle in reverse. As brand manager succeeds brand manager, the one with the least vested interest in the product is entrusted with the brand. In another typical scenario, the brand manager neglects to update the product to fit changing lifestyles or competitive situations once it loses its initial momentum.

This boredom is reflected on the shelf and to the consumer. Colgate-Palmolive's Ajax brand is a product line that failed to acknowledge changing market conditions. Before its recent updating, the line of products looked like a lost child of the pre-Beatles 1960s. Now it looks good on the shelf, but its "value" advertising made it an afterthought to consumers.

In marketing to children, there is an axiom that the market renews itself every eight years. If we extend that concept into the adult world, there are continuing and changing marketing opportunities as demographic groups naturally evolve and segment themselves. For instance, a girl's needs get closer to her mother's as she enters her twenties. This new closeness gives you a new opportunity to sell to her because her values and product choices change, in keeping with her new adult role. She no longer wants the products she used as a teenager, but she often wants the ones that served her mother so well.

In the continual search for new products, the big marketing opportunity might be the product you've been ignoring all these years because you thought it was in its death throes, which were, in fact, self-imposed.

There are usually three symptoms of a neglected product:

1. The product is positioned with a value/price strategy (as if it's a unique idea).

2. Product advertising, if the product is supported at all, carries a prominent picture of the American flag.

3. For lack of a better idea, the product is given a logical, reason-why appeal, which is rejected by consumers. For some reason, when a company can't think of anything else to say about a product, it conducts a taste test—which consumers usually don't find credible. Maxwell House, a few years back, conducted a very silly taste test campaign with none other than Linda Ellerbee (who must have needed the money) that was devoid of any creative thought. Compare this with Starbucks, which reenergized the coffee market with new flavors and a style all its own.

The good news is that you can liven up products that have downtrending or stagnant sales patterns.

Two products that were, until recently, in vital need of new energy were the previously mentioned Ajax cleaning line and Herbal Essence, a monster shampoo in the 1970s. Finally, after years of not-so-benign neglect, Colgate is trying to establish a younger lifestyle repositioning after its ill-conceived, throwaway price/value campaign of a short time ago. Clairol has also livened up Herbal Essence for newly identified market segments. It has met with a great success.

On another front, honey cooperatives are in a tizzy because they feel that the product's golden time in the 1970s has past. Honey is a product category that is ripe for positioning and marketing innovations by the honey cooperatives. Look at the fantastic job done by the raisin cooperatives and the Ocean Spray Cranberry group.

In the next chapter, we're going to explore specifics on how to reverse the fortunes of stagnant brands. But it's important to realize that brands often flatline because of the emotional state of the manager or company that's in charge of the brand. The brand is treated as old hat or past its prime. Nobody wants to take on the challenge of straightening it out. Managers jump at the myth of the product life cycle because it's the easy way out. Developing a new product is fun and glamorous. Marketers see an old product as boring, and this boredom is transferred to the product in the form of few changes in packaging or marketing strategy.

A simple way of getting around this ennui is to pretend that this is a new product.

You can interfere with the downward momentum of so-called product life cycle by treating the product as you would a new product launch. After all, when you reposition a product, you are creating a new spot in consumers' minds. But be careful not to forget what the original product brought to the consumer party. Create a new Share of Heart that combines the old and the new. New, updated packaging. New applicators. New applications. New scents. Murphy soap (owned by Colgate-Palmolive), Jell-O, even Cheez Whiz and Velveeta have shattered the myth of the product life cycle because they've been periodically reviewed and allowed to evolve to fit in with the changing times. Look at Cheerios. In our generation alone it's gone from a kids' cereal—it's got "Go Power" (I never did figure why they made 'em like little O's)—to a staple of a more mature market, capitalizing on the grains-are-good-for-you trend . . . without missing a beat. Line extensions keep the brand vibrant and profitable.

Add Share of Heart by attaching new uses to your product. Consumers love to discover applications for the tried and true. New fabrics, new home surfaces, new ways of eating and doing business all provide new repositioning opportunities for these old reliables. Go after new consumer segments. Now that I've said that, whole industries do become mature and need to change. Just a short ten years ago, typesetting was a strong industry. Then computers came in, and now almost every advertising agency and magazine publisher is its own typesetter. New products and services should be developed when business is good. If you wait too long, you'll lag too far behind your competitors to do much good. As one industry comes in, another industry takes its place. It's the aware industry that plots its own course.

In the Fulton Fish Market, the prime business was distribution. For example, most sales went through the Fulton Fish Market in New York and other fish markets across the country. As better shipping modes developed, restaurants and seafood distributors could acquire their product directly. They no longer needed the expense of the Fulton Fish Market.

Smart fish marketers became value-added producers. Restaurants were sent complete fish dinners, rather than raw seafood. Fishmongers even developed better presentations for supermarkets. The supermarkets, with the fish sellers' help, made their seafood counters more appetizing. Smart sellers adopted and adapted merchandising tactics from purveyors of other commodities. Tyson Chicken now gets 85 percent of its sales from value-added products that satisfy the consumer's desire for a wholesome dinner that can be "home made" in thirty minutes or less. A good home-cooked chicken dinner is considered food for the soul. If it can be made quickly and cheaper, it can make it into the consumer's heart.

The Myth of Declining Brand Loyalty

This myth is insidious and pervasive. There is no lack of brand loyalty when the product gives consumers the same good feelings it has always given. The seeming lack of loyalty is brought on by yourself. As Pogo said, "We have met the enemy and it is us." The way many marketers treat product loyalty and their own customers is the epitome of the double standard. They philander, change the product, and keep upping the price without a consumer-driven reason, yet they want consumers to be loyal. A fascinating contradiction is that the same managers who complain about lack of brand loyalty keep offering new, but soggy, line extensions. Product and brand loyalty have to be earned on an everyday basis. You have to earn product loyalty by continually doing something nice for your customers and by reminding them how important the product is to their lives.

Emotional involvement is what builds brand loyalty. Most purchases are made because we think the product will make our lives a little happier, will make us more powerful, more feminine, or more efficient. It's important to let your customer know that you are doing this. If you neglect to reinforce the warm feelings, you lose loyalty. When you show consumers that they made the correct purchase decision, they will buy your product or service again and again.

An interesting phenomenon that is seen in interactive consumer groups is that consumers are growing more and more skeptical about products in general. Many consumers feel that there is less and less of the active ingredients in the products they're buying. They feel that the products are changing behind their backs. And, as we all know, they're right. There is a tremendous lack of loyalty to consumers. This is partly due to the megamergers and buyouts.

In the Northeast, Freihoffer Bakeries was purchased by General Foods with nary a mention in the newspapers. In fact, there was no mention of GF on the package. But the "flagship" bread was changed. The product was not the same one that consumers loved for years. When sales of the bread flattened, could we blame it on declining loyalty? You change the brand, confuse consumers, put in cheaper ingredients, then complain about declining brand loyalty? Give me a break! Care about your customers and they'll care about you. Don't make changes and hope for the best. If you must change the product, change it in a way that consumers want.

Manufacturers are not giving consumers anything to be loyal about. Cereal manufacturers recently charged five bucks a pop for a box of cereal and then wondered why consumers switched to the store brands. Keep infusing your brands with a Share of Heart along with a price break and watch the consumers come running. A better product for less money is a sure way to build loyalty. Most people would buy name brands if they had the money, but they don't want to take out a bank loan for a box of Rice Krispies.

Where there's a need, there's a market. Malt-O-Meal, a cereal manufacturer with no "killer" brands, now develops knockoffs of popular cereals at budget prices. In doing so, it is revitalizing its own brand name and creating new equities. Malt-O-Meal's choice of polyethylene bags rather than the standard box is another key difference. It separates Malt-O-Meal's product from the other, boxed products on the shelf. Consumers know they're paying for a Cocoa Puffs clone and that the packaging is not adding to the price. They feel smart for making the purchase. Give Malt-O-Meal a great deal of credit for finding a niche and filling it well, which can be tough for an old-line brand name that is used to doing things the way they've always been done.

Surprisingly, the Europeans knew about building brands long before we did. In Great Britain, private label, which can definitely be considered a branding technique, is king. Some private-label products hold a forty to fifty share of market. Other brands are featured as afterthoughts. That's because retailers there instill the class and prestige of their store into the product as if it were an integral part of the shop.

When you see a product or product category that has been abandoned because of the alleged marketing truisms, it's time to seize the moment. Infuse your brands with emotion, fun, and prestige. That's the way to build and keep brand loyalty. Stake out your territory and guard it with the ardor of a new-found lover.

Just like a fingerprint, every product and service is unique. The alleged marketing truisms just don't count anymore (as if they ever did).

The Myth of the Parity or Low-Interest Product

One of the marketing person's allegedly most difficult jobs is building a share of market for a so-called parity product—one that has no apparent advantage over existing products.

I don't believe there are parity products. There are only lazy marketers. Parity products are just stock keeping units (SKUs) that haven't staked out emotional or physical footprints that differentiate themselves on the shelf. Let's take butter, for example. All butters are the same, aren't they? But a solid marketer like Land O' Lakes can come up with several flanking products with their own set of consumer benefits. There's even a new butter with 50 percent more butterfat than competing products. Follow-the-leader and me-too brands should have a life of their own rather than just achieving a parity status. Wal-Mart has done a sterling job with its store brands.

There is no such thing as a parity product as long as consumers have to make choices. Consumers must make value judgments about each product they choose. And various studies show that they give your product about thirty seconds at most.

But some products magically succeed in building and maintaining share dominance while others face the prospect of playing follow the leader. Watch a customer make a buying decision about a so-called parity product, like American cheese. Watch

him or her pick up a product, then put it down. Watch him or her compare labels and prices. To the customer, there's a difference between identical products. Every consumer product has its own emotional fingerprint.

You can differentiate your product by giving it a new function that the other guy hasn't thought of yet. This makes consumers feel clever, like they're getting something for nothing. Become a hero for solving two problems for the cost of one. Arm & Hammer baking soda, of course, is a great example of building a consumer base from a common product. Now consumers buy two boxes—one for general use and one as a refrigerator deodorant.

Despite the consumer-driven benefits of a low price, you can define your product's uniqueness by charging slightly more. Yes, more. Make your product stand out from the crowd by giving it a premium image. Make it so prestigious that consumers have to sacrifice by paying more to get it. It will often be valued more.

Try making a minor cosmetic change, but tie it into the emotional value of the product. Frank Perdue created an upheaval in the chicken business when he capitalized on the fact that his chickens had a brand name and yellow skin. This convinced consumers that Perdue chickens were healthier, prime chickens. They seemed healthier to consumers because Perdue positioned himself as an expert and said yellow was better.

Give your product a new name that consumers either love or hate. Stay away from neutral names with no emotional value. Bully toilet bowl cleaner arouses negatives, but to consumers, it sounds as if it will really work. Snuggle is a great name for a fabric softener, especially when it's positioned for kids' clothes.

Hotel Bar butter, Glad storage bags, Ronzoni pasta, Evian water, and Absolut vodka are all products that succeed despite a so-called parity environment. Consumers feel that they are buying the best—and if they can afford it, why shouldn't they? It's an affordable luxury. There's a whole new paradigm driven by consumer dynamics. Consumers are gravitating toward premium brands with substance and image as they never have before.

To most lettuce growers, lettuce is a parity product in a commodity category. At least, it was until Foxy lettuce decided to change the playing field. Foxy inserted its lettuce heads into individual plastic bags, with the name *Foxy* in big type. Consumers felt that they were getting a product that had not been picked over by shoppers. Foxy lettuce sales soared. The plastic bag and brand name conveyed trust and confidence. The new look also caused supermarket buyers to specify Foxy over competing no-name products. Foxy is now building on its newly developed equity to sell prepared salads, to excellent consumer—and supermarket—reception.

Suntan lotions with government-mandated SPF (sun protection factor) numbers should be so-called parity products, but they're a hotbed of marketing opportunities and positionings. Coppertone has taken its famous ad and developed a product around the symbol—Waterbabies. It plays on the nurturing motivation. The product stands out and invites purchase. It has a hefty price tag, but it beats rubbing Noxzema on a screaming, hurt child after a hot time in the sun. The whole sunscreen category is a textbook example of creative marketers (and some not-so-creative marketers) differentiating their products in a parity environment.

There is no such thing as a low-interest product. There are only disinterested, uninvolved marketers. This marketing myth is self-fulfilling and destructive. It's the opposite of what marketing to the heart should be.

How to Beat the System: Positioning Your Product in a Changing Market

You can ignore all these marketing myths when you monitor your brands and go for the heart. There is one truism that can't be debated: Your customers are always evolving. What made them happy yesterday may not make them happy today. New needs are forever arising.

A change in your customers' brand commitment is due to emotional or *positioning obsolescence*. The product no longer resonates in the consumers' heads or hearts. Your customers' expectations have gradually changed. They have moved on to new experiences. In a business-to-business situation, your customer may have stopped using your services because you didn't give him or her any reason to remember you—you didn't reinforce your importance. The product or positioning has less meaning than it had before. The market has passed you by.

There are a great many brands and products that can usurp your positioning or come up with an even better selling proposition. You and your product will be replaced if you don't keep enhancing it.

Examples abound:

Snapple. It was the beverage of the early 1990s. Its unique flavors and advertising gave it a special appeal to young adults. Then Quaker Foods bought the brand and could no longer keep the product as unique as its former owners had done. Quaker had no clue to the product's appeal—but the brand name probably looked great on Quaker's spreadsheets. Snapple's market share has been eroded by Mistic beverages, AriZona beverages, Fruitopia, and Nantucket Nectars—offbeat products that Snapple itself spawned.

Kmart. This is a flagrant example of a company that did not keep up with the times. Kmart was a leading discount store until it was undermined by Wal-Mart. Kmart has lost its way, its positioning, and its customers. Its last commercials featured Penny Marshall and Rosie O'Donnell acting obnoxiously. There was no point to these commercials. It was almost embarrassing to walk into a Kmart after Penny and Rosie trashed it. Compare this with Wal-Mart's Share of Heart. Said a rival retailer on the strength of Wal-Mart, "Even when their pricing and selection isn't any better than ours, consumers make the purchase at Wal-Mart's instead of us."

Fayva Shoes. This company was first on the block with discount shoes, then neglected to tweak its image when additional discount shoe peddlers, mainly Payless Shoe Source, came by.

CompuServe and Prodigy. They owned the computer on-line service business until America Online, with its ultrapowerful "community" positioning, darted past both of them. CompuServe, despite a ten-year head start in the business, was considered too complicated for the average user. The company was too stiff-necked to react to market changes. Prodigy had stodgy graphics and weak content. AOL is constantly improving, not resting on its laurels, and is continually building on its strengths (so much so that it recently attracted an overwhelming number of sign-ups, which taxed resources).

It's imperative to stop positioning obsolescence before it begins. To paraphrase Robin Williams in the movie *Dead Poets Society*, you have to seize the moment.

The bottled water category is a case study of beating positioning obsolescence. Favored bottled water brands change more quickly than monthly selections from the Book-of-the-Month Club. To combat this fickleness, some savvy water marketers change their brand's name and packaging every six months or so. They restage products even before the product starts losing steam.

Restaging, or repositioning (in the classic sense, anyway), uses advertising and promotional tools. But the positioning should be manifested in the packaging and the product itself. The product should be as unique and exciting as it originally was. Share of Heart should help you to differentiate your product all the way down to the point of sale.

Consumer mind-sets are continually changing. You have to find out about those changes, because nobody will tell you about them.

The Ring Ding Evolution Opportunity

Back in the mid-1930s, a unique product was invented. It would soon set the world on its ears and be vilified as an example of decadent America the world over. But its ramifications would be felt in modern-day marketing, and the basic principles of its ultrasophisticated marketing strategy would never change, for it was the grandfather of the Dove Bar.

The Ring Ding (for you midwesterners out there, the Ding Dong) belongs in the marketing hall of fame. A direct descendent of the hockey puck, it was (and still is) a chocolate orb filled with an ersatz white cream that came clad in crinkly cellophane and that, on warm days, left a gooey chocolatey mess on its cardboard platter that was a whole lot of fun to lick off. It didn't even have microwave directions.

It had only a single redeeming quality, which was foremost in the mind of the typical twelve-year-old: It tasted good. To kids, it was a luxury and worth the price. We didn't expect it to turn us into Superman or even supply us with one third of the minimum daily requirement of anything.

We've grown up. Or have we?

Adults will still choose something that tastes good over something that's good for them. Just as we eagerly anticipated the taste of a Ring Ding, we now anticipate the taste of a gourmet ice cream. There is a trend toward gourmet products, even those that have a thoroughly unhealthy image.

The common marketing wisdom is that we're a nation of health-conscious adults, torturing ourselves on Nautilus machines, scrutinizing labels for any hint of the devil cholesterol, and eschewing anything related to junk foods. So this is heady stuff to marketers who accept this wisdom.

The common marketing wisdom is misguided. Our tastes have simply grown up. We've evolved from Ring Dings to Ben & Jerry's New York Super Fudge Chunk. We've gone from macaroni and cheese to fettuccine alfredo. From wieners to wiener schnitzel.

If the 1970s and early 1980s were a period of product have-nots (no preservatives, no caffeine, no artificial anythings), we are entering a period of haves—more chocolate, more real butterfat, more natural ingredients. We have not substituted good nutrition for good taste, although we will compromise now and then.

Take Dove Bars, for example. When Dove Bars came onto the scene, they were ridiculed in some quarters because "savvy" marketers doubted that consumers would pay two dollars for an ice cream bar when perfectly serviceable ice cream bars cost about fifty cents. Dove Bars, like other category mavericks, simply redefined the product and what consumers would pay for it.

We've moved on to better things, and the money we are willing to spend on them has increased proportionally. With theater tickets being priced at $75 and tickets to rock concerts regularly scalped at $250, people don't find $2 too much to pay to satisfy an impulse for upscale gratification.

The junk foods of yesterday have evolved into the gourmet products of today. The Dove Bar is a Ring Ding, all grown up.

People have redefined what they are willing to pay to satisfy themselves. While paying two dollars may have seemed sinful the first time, consumers rapidly take price increases in stride. (But only when you have gratified them. Five bucks for an ordinary box of cereal is still too much—there's little emotional gratification in breakfast foods.)

Not only are they willing to pay it, they expect to pay it. It's all part of consumer evolution.

Today's adults are the first generation to grow up with supermarkets and television. When we talk about home cooking, we probably mean something that came from a can or a freezer. The standard of identity has changed. Campbell's is the standard of identity for soup, jarred sauces are the standard of identity for spaghetti sauce. And the McDonald's counterfeit shake has changed the way we think about a milk shake.

In almost every category an inspired marketer has taken a basic product and attached a higher price.

It's amazing what you can do when you ignore the textbook, play to the consumers' hearts, and stretch the creative envelope. Comedian Lenny Bruce used to brag that when he was a kid, he used to sell eggs with something extra—chicken manure. Traveling tourists would think the eggs were just laid fresh and would gladly pay more for them. (That's the reason farmers often, and purposely, write their signs with letters that are backwards. Roadside customers like to think they're buying from an ignorant rube.)

Many marketers position their products for the mass market mentality. It's the toughest route because it lumps you with your competition. Use product strategy to separate your product on the shelf and in their hearts.

It works the same way for banks as for packaged goods. NatWest U.S.A. undertook a program to increase its mortgage business among real estate brokers in the New York metropolitan area. It was competing with a large number of firmly entrenched, aggressive mortgage providers and felt that it needed additional strengths, particularly when key players were offering rebates (i.e., bribes) to real estate brokers. NatWest wanted to determine the strategic directions it could take to make inroads with real estate brokers. It wanted a breakthrough marketing strategy.

The breakthrough strategy came down to one word, *relationships*. Brokers wanted to know that NatWest would stand by their side and hold their hands until the mortgage came through. No discounts. No "lowest rate." They just wanted their bank to love them.

By the way, the Ring Ding is still going strong, only now it's got sprayed-on vitamins and minerals to appease General Mom.

It's Up to You

There are many excuses you can make for declining market share. But most of the reasons for market declines are self-inflicted—not learning about the customer and not changing with the times. Markets are there for the taking when you update your marketing programs to keep consumers involved.

How Marketing to the Heart Can Reverse the Fortunes of Stagnant or Declining Brands

If the cola wars ever become the root-beer wars, Barq's root beer is going to be a major instigator. Louisiana has never been known as a hotbed of free enterprise on a national scale. Most of the companies there do business within the good old boy network of the Gulf states. Barq's root beer was a regional player, too, for over eighty years, and it was in decline until it was bought by the team of John Oudt and John Koerner. They transformed the regional, stagnant beverage into a significant national brand. It is only subject to argument as to who is the number two root beer maker in the United States, Barq's or Pepsi (A&W is number one).

At the time Oudt and Koerner took over Barq's, Coke and Pepsi were fighting their cola wars. Advertising alone cost the two of them $150 million per year. Like Robin Sommers with American Spirit cigarettes, Oudt and Koerner figured that the big guns' attention would be diverted from the much smaller market. Like Sommers, they were right.

The key part of their success story is how they merchandised the brand and built a new Share of Heart. While the package and promotion for Pepsi's Mug root beer sported the traditional handlebar mustache and Gay Nineties theme,

Barq's broke the rules. Nostalgia was out—good times was the message.

"Our target is under twenty-four," says Koerner. "We do things that Pepsi wouldn't because it offends their large consumer base." That includes advertising on MTV and a rock thing called the Head Banger's Ball, where it sponsored the rock group Anthrax. It also created an off-the-wall Match-Your-DNA promotion and gave away a bunch of Russian trinkets when the Soviet Union broke up. These were all very un-root-beer-like. The product's formulation is different from Mug's too—it has caffeine to give the user a quick energy jolt.

Koerner and Oudt took a declining business and made it work by understanding and finely focusing on their market's emotional pulls and the lack of motivation by competing companies.

Brands Wanted—Dead or (Barely) Alive

There is a morbid game that people play called Dead or Alive. One person mentions a celebrity and the other has to say whether that person is dead or alive. You can play the game with products and brands too. Which brands still exist: 7-Up Gold, Dodge Dart, Uneeda Biscuit, Maypo, Wheatena, Bon Ami, Rinso, Bosco, Old Gold cigarettes?

The dead products are 7-Up Gold and the Dodge Dart. All of these brands, however, are victims of positioning obsolescence. Their positioning and product benefits were once on target, but they were no longer perceived by their companies' management to have the same consumer pull they had once had. Management considered them past their prime and neglected them, either purposely or by happenstance.

When customers fall out of love with a product, it is usually gradual. They may have found a product that looked a little flashier, was advertised a little better, or offered them a slightly better benefit. With business-to-business products, someone new and persuasive might have walked through the door while you weren't looking. In any event, loss of customer appeal usually occurs little by little. Management may not be aware of what is happening. But a slight drop in market appeal here and there can lead to a precipitous decline.

When the decline becomes steep, the corporate knee-jerk reaction is either to milk the brand for all it's worth—and hasten its death—or to kill it off with a shotgun blast to the head. Bang, you're dead. Hasta la vista. That's what the business books say you should do, anyway.

But, to paraphrase a great commercial, a (once-compelling) brand is a terrible thing to waste. It's usually a lot more economical and fruitful to restage a product than to send it out to wherever a brand goes when it dies. And restagings are definitely cheaper and more efficient than building brands from scratch. In a business-to-business situation, it's easier to reinvent yourself and sell more services because you already have your foot in the door—the toughest part of making the sale. Repositioning is simply rebonding with your customer. Your task is to get into your customer's heart again. Many brands or products can be revitalized by infusing them with emotion and backing this up with reason to fit in changing markets. It's like the old Jewish comedians—they changed their names and made their shtick more mainstream to fit in with broad Gentile audiences. In essence, they remade themselves. When you reposition a product, you're basically reinventing it.

Requirements for Repositioning

In order to be revitalized, the brand or service should have several things going for it:

▷ The brand should have strong emotional equities that can be recognized by a core group of consumers. These are the customers that are going to drive your product's initial sales.

▷ The brand may have slid down in the marketplace, but it should still be selling steadily to a targetable base. If the brand doesn't stand for something concrete in the consumer's mind, you might as well start from scratch with a new brand or product. In a business-to-business situation, if the customer doesn't like you or respect you personally, you're not going to get back through the door—you may get to the lobby, but you won't reach the sacred conference room.

▷ The brand should have been a reasonably strong seller in its time, preferably one of the top three in its category. It should have had a distinctive emotional or rational point of difference.

▷ The brand should never have been given a value positioning. Once you lower the price of a product and make it a budget brand, it loses its emotional equity. The Commodore 64 computer was once the largest-selling home computer in the United States. Then it lost its market share to faster computers—those with a more professional presence. Commodore's problem was that it never developed bragging rights. Its lack of a strong, identifiable image as a state-of-the-art computer hurt it. And now the lack of a strong brand image prevents any reworking of the brand.

Lorillard has sent Old Gold cigarettes to the scrap heap by making it a value brand. It could have successfully repositioned the product as an all-natural product to combat American Spirit. At the very least, Lorillard could have battled the all-natural American Spirit positioning by reformulating the brand.

▷ Management should have a strong emotional commitment to restaging the brand. If management isn't passionate about the product or relegates the task to a young marketer without a strong track record, they're going to fight the restaging any time they are asked for resources. Often, companies that loudly proclaim that they're changing their products because of "the customer-driven revolution" settle for just a minor cosmetic change, like an "improved" banner on the label. When this doesn't work (and it usually doesn't), they write the brand off, saying, "Well, we tried."

Change is not easy. It's painful. You're making major changes in what might have been hallowed ground. Until fairly recently, Coca-Cola management would not use the Coke name on any product but its flagship brand. Now there's Diet Coke, Cherry Coke, Caffeine Free Coke, and a whole slew of other names too numerous to mention here. And they all have their unique emotional pulls.

Tools of Repositioning

Most people, when they talk about repositioning, are talking about advertising and promotion. Those are just two tools of repositioning to the heart. Here are ten ways to revitalize or reposition a product so that it appeals to the heart.

1. Change the product.
2. Line up line extensions.
3. Change the name.
4. Change the name and the product.
5. Add a new use.
6. Go after new emotional equities.
7. Change your selling outlets and your customer profiles.
8. Change the rules.
9. Borrow someone else's emotional equities.
10. Just say *new* (but mean it).

The goal is to change your customers' perception of your product and make it more meaningful to a critical mass of consumers.

You may have to take the brand apart completely and eviscerate it. Chances are the brand was neglected and left to rot like a tooth cavity. When you drill out the decayed matter, all you may have left is the shell. In some cases, the only thing that might be left is the brand name. But don't forget, a strong brand name may be worth more than the factory that makes the product.

The process may even be emotionally distressing, for you are tearing down a brand that you and your consumers once had extremely positive feelings for. There's also a chance that you might offend or lose the sales of currently loyal customers if you don't handle the restaging correctly.

But a funny thing happens when you restage a brand. It has long-term effects on both the bottom line and company morale. The entire company rallies around what its customers want and around your brand. Few people want to be part of a declining brand or business, but everyone wants to be part of a successful turnaround. If you have to tear the product down piece by piece, you will be making a failing product whole again.

Start by choosing your candidates carefully. If yours is a one-product company, you'll have to decide if changing the product is worth the risk of losing current customers.

Learn your brand's strengths and weaknesses. Ascertain what leveraging power the brand still has. Most brand restagings leverage a brand's strengths. That sounds obvious, but you can also restage a brand by deleting negatives. This is much more difficult, for consumers remember the bad experiences they had with your product much better than they remember the positive aspects. When you took a written driver's test or an exam at school, didn't you later remember the wrong answers better than the correct ones?

Like locating your most leverageable assets, your strengths may be hard to find. They may lie in the emotion your product elicited a long time ago—even though to most marketers, a long time ago is any time before they arrived at the brand's helm.

Your strengths may be as far away as a child's memories. At a tender age, even as young as three or four, children begin building impressions of products through sensory and cognitive experiences. They react to shapes, colors, flavors, smells—and even logos. They may not be able to read the letters on the logo, but they can understand what the shape of the logo symbolizes. TV commercials also make indelible impressions on a child's psyche.

Kids remember the products that made them happy or made their parents happy. Baby boomers often remember their families' first cars—and the good times associated with them. They recall with fondness the 1955 Chevy Belair or the first Mustang.

Most kids grow up (now there's a heavy-duty insight), and they will gravitate to the products that they are familiar with. They will often choose the product their parents bought, so long as you update the product to keep it moving with the times and in tune with your customers' self-perceived role in society. The product should relate to the evolving person you're selling to.

The Fuller Brush man is associated with good times. The brand is meaningful to consumers even if door-to-door selling is passé. The Fuller Brush man's products took on almost superhuman status. By our standards, Fuller Brush is a strong candidate for repositioning.

A repositioning of an existing product can lead to sales in unexpected ways. It can actually create sales in new categories or help you start a new category.

Change the Product

Nabisco's incredible success with its SnackWell's line of fat-free products is based on a repositioning of its Devil's Food Cookie Cakes. And it's based on the self-reward hot button, with a guilt-free payoff.

Nabisco's Devil's Food Cookie Cakes had been limping on the shelf for some time. The product was not quite good enough to be considered a self-reward, yet it was too high in fat to be perceived as nutritionally sound. Sales were steady, but slow.

At the same time the brand was stagnating, all of Nabisco's divisions were uniting to develop a good-tasting, no-fat product.

When most companies embark on a massive new product development program, they choose new forms and textures. Here's where Nabisco was smart. It knew that Devil's Food Cookie Cakes offered good taste expectations, so it used the product to demonstrate its new no-fat technology. By repositioning the treat, the company provided a frame of reference to consumers. It was like a live-action technology demo. Nabisco wasn't afraid to lose sales of its existing Devil's Food Cookie Cakes product because the company knew that its SnackWell's product, now fat-free, tasted just as good as the original. The product actually caused a nationwide Fat Free Devil's Food Cookie Cakes shortage, which, while not as disastrous as a gas shortage or a Häagen Dazs shortage, elicited angry cries from consumers. That's how badly they wanted the product.

Line Up Line Extensions

Line extensions can be an efficient way to rebuild your brand's emotional leverage. Inept line extensions, on the other hand, are the fastest way to run your brand further into the ground. Poorly performing line extensions are usually the fault of misguided research into a core brand's emotional equity. This faulty research is compounded by poor design of line extensions or building line extensions on the wrong equities.

Jaws was a great movie, wasn't it? *Jaws II*, like most movie sequels, tried to parlay the brand name and unique *Jaws* imagery to create an almost new product. But by making a movie that had no strength (I've resisted the urge to say bite) of its own, the producers doomed it to capture only a portion of *Jaws'* original audience.

A sequel is the ultimate line extension, a product that relies on its parent "key" to build share. There are two differences, though. Line extensions don't usually have names like Son of Skippy or Glad-Lock III—The Opening. They can, however, often be spotted by the word *plus*, *gold*, or *lite* at the end. A more serious difference, though, is that you only have to sell a movie once. You have to reach consumers through your line extensions every time out.

As when they make plans to attend a sequel, consumers bring their own preconceived expectations of how the brand and its line extensions should perform.

Unlike a sequel, out for the fast buck, a line extension should enhance its parent brand every time out.

Line extensions have long been used to procure more shelf space, to develop more SKUs, and to utilize more of a factory's capacity. But they can, and should, be used to reestablish your relationship with your customer.

A correctly executed line extension reinforces the core brand's basic emotional and visual appeal on the shelf. Your brand and your line extensions should come together on the shelf as a complete visual unit that expresses your new image.

A mistake made by marketers is to think of line extensions as the "strawberry strategy." When a food company wants to add a line extension, the brand manager says, "Let's make it in strawberry." But a true line extension is more than just a new flavor or an added SKU. It should change the consumer's whole attitude toward your product line.

As I mentioned in the last chapter, after years of running a distant number two to Crest in the toothpaste category, Colgate acted to enhance its image through pithy line extensions.

During the period in which it was stagnating, Colgate had few new products. Crest was seen as the ultimate in dental therapeutics. But Colgate decided it wanted to be taken seriously. It did this through line extensions. Within a few years, it introduced Colgate Junior (the first "serious" toothpaste for kids and positioned to mom), Colgate with Baking Soda, Colgate with Baking Soda & Peroxide, and Colgate Tartar Control. The new line extensions broadcast a new image of Colgate to consumers. No longer was Colgate considered just an old-fashioned toothpaste—it was now a serious tooth care provider.

Line extensions reflect and add to customers' mental image of your brand. They keep it lively and updated in the hearts of consumers.

Line extensions should not be developed haphazardly. They are a serious tool in the repositioning of a brand. All line extensions should enhance the brand, not just flank the brand. All line extensions should give added emotional "oomph" to the brand.

Campbell's Franco-American division used line extensions to reposition its canned macaroni products as toys. Yes, now you're supposed to "play" with your food. It was food as fun (not fun food, which has a not-so-serious nutrition connotation).

Through Campbell's research, Franco-American found that it had strong emotional equity with moms, but not with kids—and kids were the key purchase influencers. It created Franco-American pasta line extensions with products shaped like popular images. It formed the product into shapes that roughly resembled Sonic the Hedgehog and Gargoyles. Sales skyrocketed. Kids hounded mom for the product.

But Franco-American didn't stop there. It used borrowed interest to keep the category compelling. More about its success in a few pages.

By the way, a cardinal rule in dealing with kids on an emotional level is never to make your product appeal younger than your target audience. Little kids aspire to be like the big kids, but older children will turn up their noses at any product positioned to a younger child. They consider it babyish. If your line extensions skew too young, the older kids won't buy your product. Franco-American has tiptoed this fine line very successfully.

Change the Name

Dorman's was a well-known cheesemaker on the East Coast. Among its products was a nondescript American cheese. It was a low-priced "value brand" competing against such giants as Kraft and Borden's. Because of poor sales, most supermarkets were heaving the product out of their stores.

Dorman's looked at its options. It could stop making the product (kill the brand) or cut prices even lower. Or, because it had a strong presence in deli departments, it could sell the cheese in bulk to be fresh sliced. The problem was that deli departments offered small profit margins. Also, people didn't like the long lines typical at the deli counter.

So we ran interactive groups for Dorman's. It turned out that most American cheese was bought for children. There was none positioned for the adults in the house.

So we left the product as it was and came up with the name Deli Singles. It was now positioned for adults: "Deli Taste without the Wait." Dorman's increased the price a half dollar to demonstrate that the product was special. The moves turned the product around. The cheese is still nondescript-tasting, but Dorman's Deli Singles has been selling well for over a decade now.

Unbeknownst to many, there are two main parts to a brand name. There is the glamorous *name*. It beckons from the shelf or an ad, boldly proclaiming, "Buy me. Take me, I'm yours!" Then there is the poor, lowly *descriptor* that describes what the product is for. No one pays much attention to it. It's just put there as an afterthought.

But sometimes just changing the descriptor is enough to drive new sales. Marketers are told that consumers get most of their product information through advertising. That's not entirely true. While advertising can be the first step in providing imagery and an overall view of the product, most products and brands are decided upon at the place of purchase.

The descriptor can alter the way consumers feel that the product will help them. It is a vital usage cue for consumers. Changing the descriptor changes the way consumers relate to the product.

Several flour companies have jumped on the bread machine bandwagon. The major change in their product is the descriptor

"Ideal for Bread Machines." It's simple. But when consumers are investing four hours to make bread and have this prestigious-brand machine, why should they take chances?

Change the Name and the Product

But what if your brand has no clear strengths? What if your company is not highly thought of? What if your Share of Heart is negative? It's sad. It happens. It's common.

First, of course, look deeper into your product through consumer research to find something unique. But if you still can't find anything worthwhile, all is not lost. The solution: Hide yourself. Then remake yourself with a new Share of Heart. Pretend this is a new company. Cast off all the negative vibrations. Completely revamp the product—the name, the colors, and the product form. This sounds drastic, but is it? You still have the factory and the know-how. You're simply eliminating your unwanted consumer baggage. If you were Commodore, would you introduce a new computer using the Commodore brand name, given consumer perceptions that your product was old? No; you would come up with a new product, dramatize the technology, and reinvent yourself with a new name.

When you engage in a total product/positioning overhaul, handle it the way you would a new product. The positioning and the product benefits should be determined at the initial stages and should determine most aspects of the product. Your new product should be engineered around your new positioning strategy. Since you have probably been in business for a while, you probably know your customers' motivations. If you don't know them, learn them. Build your products around them. Chances are you even have an extensive archive of products that were ahead of their time. Now may be the time to produce them, for consumers have changed.

Let's assume that you now have a product positioning that looks as if it will be well received by consumers. If you did your concept probe homework well enough, you know why consumers want the product, and even what they would pay for it. And you know the competition's strengths and weaknesses. You're now ready to capture a new market or reacquaint yourself with your old market.

I'm sure you've seen the ads for the Dirt Devil vacuum cleaner. The product is bright red and looks like no other vacuum cleaner on the market. It's a leading seller, too.

So, is the Dirt Devil a new product, made for twenty-first-century dirt?

No. It's made by Royal, an appliance company that has been around seemingly forever. The company decided that the Royal name was weak, its brand imagery was weak, and consumers didn't think much of its product line. The brand needed a complete overhaul. Because of this negative consumer equity in its corporate appellation, Royal downplayed its corporate origin. It reinvented the vacuum cleaner, jazzed it up for people who wanted to buy the best that could be bought—and created a huge market. Like Dracula, the company came back from the dead—because of a positioning that played to the heart, the positioning of power to control the toughest dirt.

Add a New Use

Give your product a new meaning by giving it a new use.

It should be axiomatic that you're not selling products to consumers, you're providing services. You can restage your product by providing new services—both physical and emotional. When you provide a new service to consumers, your product is more meaningful and takes on new importance to the heart.

However well your product was once positioned, consumers are constantly updating themselves. They're finding new products that satisfy them in new ways. A competitor may have launched a new product that cut into your Share of Heart. Or your customers' needs may have shifted, leaving your product a solution without a problem to solve.

Create a new problem that your product can solve. The hot button of discovery works here. People love to find new uses for existing products and love to recommend them to their friends.

There are many upset stomachs in America—probably from consuming all those SnackWell's, Coke hybrids, and Ring Dings. There are also a great many antacids. As this is being written, Zantac, Pepcid AC, and other formerly prescription stomach acid blockers are taking the lion's share of the venerable antacid category. Their positioning is strong and unique: stopping stomach aches before they begin. With these products, you ingest the product before you eat the food that disagrees with you. Now, it may seem irrational to eat foods that have the potential to wreak havoc with your innards, but that's the real, illogical consumer world out there.

Because of the success of the acid blockers, Tums changed the playing field. It entered women's hearts a new way—with the promise of calcium. Tums has always been made with calcium carbonate, and it is debatable whether the small amount of calcium that Tums provides is of any importance. But women think it's a good, free source of calcium, since they already have the upset stomach and need the antacid.

Go After New Emotional Equities

Some product and service categories are saturated with competition. Needs have been met perfectly. Your product cannot possibly be any better or solve a physical need better than anyone else's. That means it's time to create new emotional equities.

Wet Ones are disposable wipes, impregnated with a gentle soap. They were originally sold to replace toilet paper, but consumers thought toilet paper did its job pretty well. So Wet Ones went after a new market: baby care. For most mothers, their baby's cleanliness is paramount. And, of course, cleaning a baby is a messy job. So Wet Ones was repositioned to make babies as clean as can be—gently and softly. Graphics convey softness and affection.

A great many companies have tried to commercialize premoistened cleaning wipes for the consumer market. Dow Chemical introduced a line for the home. It failed to sell, except sporadically. The product created confusion. If you have a wet wipe, can you use it to clean up wet spills? Can you use it with other cleaners? Will it dry up? Can you reuse the product? (If you can't, it's pretty expensive.) Wet Ones would have been another loser in the category if it weren't for its preemptive play to the heart.

This is important in services, too. Let's say you provide office services, including typing. At one time, your competition may have been the many typing services in your area. Now, your competition is likely to be word processing software. When your competition was other typists, your selling point might have been faster, more accurate turnaround. Now that your competition is software, you can base your Share of Heart on your knowledge of your customer's business. No software program is as smart as you are.

Change Your Selling Outlets and Your Customer Profiles

Seek out new niches, new regions, and new user segments that will provide new users for your brand. A brand or product is new to anyone who hasn't seen it before.

We've been talking a great deal about computers and packaged goods, but let's get into the nuts and bolts of repositioning. I mean, let's talk about how we can reposition down-and-dirty nuts and bolts. And screws. And condoms.

It starts with a simple notion: Certain products are meant to be purchased by females, and certain products are meant to be purchased by males. Females are intimidated by hardware stores, just as males are made uncomfortable by lingerie shops and feminine hygiene departments.

Nuts and bolts manufacturers used to sell only to industrial manufacturers and hardware stores. But there were profits to be picked up at the supermarket.

One important thing to do when going from one niche to another is to learn the jargon of the niche. Buyers need to feel confident that you know their business and can relate to them.

When you go from an industrial market to a consumer market, forget the industrial market's jargon. Deal with consumers on their own terms. If you can sell nails by the pound for industrial sites, you can put a "Helping Hand" and a modern-day woman on the package and save the day for a woman who's in need of a nail. If she owns a hammer (another marketing opportunity?), she feels that she can do it.

Banks are going on-line, and the reason customers choose on-line banking is less convenience than one might think. Instead of undertaking the chore of writing checks, keeping track, and tearing the house down in search of stamps to mail them, customers have a new high-tech toy. Paying bills can be almost fun.

Turning a positive into a negative can be as simple as changing the product's placement in the store. When Ocean Spray's Cran-Orange drink was introduced, it was located in the store near orange juice. While tests showed that consumers liked it better than orange juice, the fact that it had cranberries was perceived as negative. People liked their orange juice straight. The solution: Place it near the other juices, position it as a "change of pace" beverage, and promote new usage occasions.

So what about condoms? They're not behind the drugstore counter anymore where teenage boys had to sheepishly ask for them. Now they're being sold out in the open in colorful displays in every supermarket. Because of the new ways of distributing them, new purchasers have emerged: women. Women now purchase about a third of all condoms—the hot button is security and safe fun.

Change the Rules

Barq's management created a strong product by breaking the alleged root-beer rules.

The assumptions that we make about a solution go a long way to limit the types of product/positioning changes we can make. To change the rules, you have to examine your preconceived notions to find out if they are really valid.

Thinking this way can set your mind—and your product strategies—free to venture into new, uncharted territories. Often, managers get used to thinking that things are a certain way, they've always been that way, and they will always be that way.

ConAgra's Banquet entrées, pot pies, and desserts have long been marketed as value-driven, budget products. The ingredients were not up to par with those in newly positioned frozen entrees. Line extensions were little better than the core brand's image.

Now ConAgra is trying to heighten its consumer presence with new line extensions that reflect a better product. The company is not so much changing its budget strategy as making a push for a strong family orientation. It is using the hot button of the family meal to tie all Banquet's products together. The new products strive to be the 1990s version of the home-cooked family dinner.

The company is developing preemptive, seminal products and positionings for Banquet with motivating consumer appeal—which will expand Banquet's sales and customer base significantly.

Get rid of the preconceived notion. Break the rules. Show Michelina's that it isn't the only company that can make a tasty budget entree with good ingredients.

Borrow Someone Else's Emotional Equities

Wouldn't it be great if we could be as savvy a marketer as Nike, as personable and talented as Michael Jordon, as established as Kraft, and as loved as Disney?

If you can't own them, maybe you can borrow a cup of equity from them.

Sears has used Bob Vila, formerly host of the TV home improvement program *This Old House*, to perfection. Craftsman tools and Sears home decorating products were considered good, if not great, products. Their image was getting a bit frayed around the edges, and Japanese and American companies were introducing new, cutting-edge, lightweight tools. It was going to take more than Craftman's strong guarantee to sell them. Sears chose Bob Vila, hoping to borrow a little bit of his personality and pleasing manner. The campaign is strong. Craftsman has recovered a great deal of the consumer equity that it once had because Vila is perceived as the knowledgeable, cheerful Master Builder.

Research your helpmates thoroughly and you can find out their true emotionally leverageable equities.

There are about two hundred NBA players. Every one of the players has a sneaker endorsement. Nike and other sneaker manufacturers know the importance of this borrowed interest. Most of the NBA players are African American. All the sneaker companies know that African Americans have major influence over the sneaker markets. In fact, British Knights, an English sneaker company, developed a reverse equity. Its products were accepted by the white middle class. African Americans abandoned the brand. And because African Americans no longer used it, the brand was not considered trend-setting.

Franco-American also used borrowed interest to shore up its SpaghettiOs. It created Gargoyles and Lion King on-pack tattoos to keep up the kids' image of the brand. This stimulated sales of the core SpaghettiOs brand. Because the tattoos were on the pack, they offered kids instant gratification.

One of the most important success factors in choosing your borrowed interest strategy is choosing your partner carefully. Make sure your partner's emotional assets are totally in sync with your own. Emotional mismatches will actually confuse your customers.

Just Say **New** *and Mean It*

New is a fascinating word. People love new brands and new products. But the word *new* can also be used as an eraser, eliminating past negatives—things your product has done wrong in the past or not done in the past—provided they're not too heinous. Post the word *new* on a formerly disappointing restaurant and many people will give it a second chance. Post the word *new* on any of the products in the dead-or-alive category and you will sufficiently pique many customers' interest.

If your brand is old, people will try it again. If your brand is not known, people will try it for the first time. Now, there are government regulations that say that you can use the word *new* on your package for a maximum of six months. But you can get around these regulations with small, consumer-wanted updates that help you defend the word *new* on the package. Bosco might be seen as "New Bosco—with Vitamins." "New Wheatena—now in individual portion packs." "New Old Gold—all natural." It's also important to make cosmetic updates to your package to keep your product at the forefront.

The word *new* is powerful. Used correctly, it can give a new feeling and lead to new sales for your product. And isn't that why you're reading this chapter?

What About Advertising?

You may have noticed that I've mentioned advertising only occasionally. That's because many marketers treat positioning strategy as a mystifying deity, to be dealt with only by advertising agency oracles who speak mysterious tongues. But true, effective product positioning is an integral part of the product itself. Share of Heart is the essential part of the creative marketing mix. Advertising is what most people think of when they develop brand restagings. But advertising is only one of many communications elements. Don't trust your agency. Trust your customer.

How to Do It

The goal is to learn how best to leverage through new line extensions and products. What are attractive new markets to shoot for?

If you want to achieve a larger share of your category, you should first develop insights into your consumer equity. Your brand may need additional consumer-driven leverage in order to compete more efficiently. In other words, you may need a "shot in the arm" to reach new sales levels, especially if you compete against a number of well-financed, entrenched competitors who are also staking out their claim. Explore a range of positionings that will make your name more meaningful to consumers and isolate the concept(s) that have strong preemptive market potential—that would appeal to, and expand, your customer base.

Specifically, what is your truly preemptive product difference? How should it best be leveraged? How should the product be positioned against current alternatives?

You should be developing new products that will make the brand more important in the consumer's heart, products that have strong preemptive market potential. The ideal product would appeal to, and expand beyond, your current consumer base. Benefits should be readily apparent to consumers and easily communicated on the shelf and in mass media.

You don't have to revamp your product line or call in the ad people and engineers to retool a repositioning. A good way to find the equity of your product is to put the product through its paces with interactive groups. Take your product and create ads showing different positionings. To learn the strengths of your brand versus the competition, mock up their products along with yours. Now put your logos on the competitors' ads. If consumers think theirs are stronger, you have much work to do. Also put your logo on a range of other products near your category. See how far you can stretch your equity.

Negatives Into Positives

In truth, all products are a yin and yang trade-off. But you can make the negatives of your new product work for you. That's the magic of marketing. When you restage a brand, you are going against different competition for the same Share of Heart. You can build markets when you turn a negative into a positive.

▶ *9*

Hooking the Heart Through Advertising

True story, as told by Jay Buettner, president of Jay Buettner Creative Copy:

"I was agonizing over trying to create a campaign for an electronics company in Stamford, Connecticut. I went down and met with them . . . they had a think-tank meeting. Finally, as a result of the meeting, I understood they wanted a macho image. So I came up with 'Going to Extremes for You.' They loved it. They took photos of a guy skyboarding through the air, with the company's logo on the skyboard for the visual.

"Problem: No continuity because a couple of weeks later the guy was doing his extreme thing for somebody else when he went splat and was killed.

"It's another example of everybody thinking they're being trendy by doing the trendiest thing, only to discover that there wasn't a company in America that wasn't doing so-called extreme games like Nike's . . . 'Just Do It!'

"Rule of thumb: By the time you want to do it because you've seen it, it's old!"

It's a morbid story, but its point is all too true. In much of today's advertising, production values rule even if there is no message. There is a great deal of form, but not a whole lot of substance. We can't all be like Nike and spend so much that the medium and the gee-whiz production techniques become the message (apologies to Marshall McLuhan). Nike has bucket-loads of cash. Most marketers don't.

At least two mega-companies—one in frozen food, the other in alcoholic beverages—have shut down their advertising completely. They dismiss it by saying that advertising simply doesn't work anymore. They're putting all their dollars into trade promotion and shoring up their distribution chains. But that's not the answer, because if they don't advertise, consumers will lose interest in their products.

Ad Agencies: Guesswork and Hype

There was an old *Twilight Zone* episode in which a person received the power to hear another person's thoughts. Here is what you'd hear if you were privy to your agency's thoughts:

What the advertising agency is saying out loud: "We put our whole staff on this proposal and worked overnight."

What it's thinking: "We copied our standard marketing jargon and clichés from last month's proposal."

What the agency is saying out loud: "We probably overkilled a bit because we wanted to be extremely accurate in our analysis."

What it's thinking: "I'm glad we used big type to take up space, and those fancy index dividers really make it look impressive."

What the agency is saying out loud: "I know the creative is right on target with your current and peripheral goals."

What it's thinking: "I hope we guessed right."

The problem of having nothing to say, even when they say it fairly well, begins with the first ad agency pitch and works its way down through the client to expensive media buys. Nor is this totally new.

The following is from a 1958 *Life* magazine article about the state of advertising in that year.

There have been months when the owners of advertising agencies have had to live with the frightening thought that a right guess about the future might make them a fortune,

while a bad guess might put them to shining shoes for a living.

Then the major advertising agencies started making their creative groups get out of their offices and interview real consumers. Learning directly from the people you're trying to sell to is still the admission ticket to successful advertising. Marlboro's Marlboro Country came to life through imagery that stemmed from these interviews. So did "Fly Now, Pay Later," from the airlines. One can even say that today's frozen entrées all sprang from insights created by Swanson's TV dinners back in the late 1950s when marketers learned to promote them on the basis of nutrition and family values rather than speed.

It's easy to knock advertising agencies. They're on a par with infomercials as easy targets for cheap shots. But agencies deserve them more and more.

More than ever, advertising/positioning is a product of guesswork. With advertising cutbacks, the agency is forced to cut even the most basic research services drastically. But the cutbacks occurred because the advertising the agencies produce is grossly ineffective. Advertising agencies base most of their advertising on guesswork. Worse, it's often backward guesswork.

The dark secret of advertising agencies is that most build the rationale and marketing plan after the creative is developed. If it was that good, they wouldn't have to sell it so hard to the companies they work for.

MTV and Extreme Games–type advertising is an easy sell to management. The graphics are lively, the music is exciting, and the jump cuts can really spice up an afternoon when the commercials are shown in an enclosed conference room on a deadly dull work day. Management, who want to feel they are in the "in" group, jump into this trendy advertising with a frenzy. "No wonder it's so expensive. Look at the number of cameras they used. And I got to watch. I even got Shaquille's autograph (for my kids of course)."

One advertiser, unimpressed with techno-pop advertising, calls it the NBC Olympic Games syndrome. According to him, NBC didn't think the games themselves were that important, so it produced sidebar after sidebar. Some agencies apparently think their client's products are dull, so they have to disguise them with confusing hand-held camera angles and overkill on production techniques.

Guessing about what will drive your market is very expensive. Once the message is in the media—or even as soon as the production bills are in—the dollars spent on it are gone.

As much as it can hurt large companies, the problem is worse with smaller companies. Writing off losses often means writing off the company.

Bad advertising is more the rule than the exception with smaller companies because of lack of up-front money for research. A good-looking commercial does not make up for the lack of a solid idea.

Does trendy advertising work? Unless you were the first or second in on the trend, not usually. The newest trend in advertising is to take a pop song and make it the focus of the product pitch. This works great for the music companies that collect royalties on the song, but it has been used so much it has become a cliché.

It's not that advertising agencies are trying to do the wrong thing; most take pride in their work. But most creative people are looking to build a flashy portfolio, tape, or reel. The emotional reason is pride. Most creative people want to direct a full-length movie or write the great American novel. Since they can't, producing a lively commercial is the next best thing.

Creative people are also looking to further their careers. Prospective employers reviewing a portfolio rarely ask, "Did the campaign work?" Instead they say, "This is exciting." If they don't like the portfolio, they say politely, "This is interesting." Never do they ask, "Did it sell the advertised product?"

Advertising agency management has a different agenda. They want to sell media. Selling media is how the agency makes money—selling products doesn't generate any income. The hard fact of life is that the business of advertising is selling advertising, not solving business problems. That's how advertising agencies make their money. It's been that way since advertising agencies got their start in the late 1800s strictly as sellers of media space.

Agencies know that it's more important to please the client than to sell products—if they don't, they won't get a chance to sell the product at all.

What about the consumers? Does anyone care? Can anyone afford not to care?

It's extremely difficult for advertising agencies to make money on proper motivational research (as outlined in Chapter 3). It's a waste of their economic resources, and they know it. Unless the campaign translates into a national rollout, they simply can't earn enough for a respectable return on investment. It's also bad for morale. Copywriters, creative directors, and art directors won't supply sufficient consumer stimuli because doing so doesn't result in finished ads to pump up their portfolios. In effect, whatever hours creative people put into research into the emotions that make someone buy your product is time taken away from career advancement.

That's why critical research and the creative work needed to develop key consumer insights is usually left to junior copywriters and art directors—if the agency does it at all.

Don't Let an Agency Train Creative People on Your Dollar

Of course it's true that there are agencies that can do a competent job on emotional matters, but they're clearly in the minority. Most agencies won't even take the time to learn how to do it properly. Some agencies will actually try to sabotage other people's work in order to save face with a client. One mega-agency sent more than a million dollars in creative and account talent to heckle a motivational consultant at the consultant's project conclusion presentation. The agency was embarrassed, for the consultant had done in three months what the agency had failed to do in a year: get at the emotions that drive the fabric softener market. The agency hadn't had the means, the know-how, or the inclination to handle the project correctly.

The old axiom attributed to many people—"half of my advertising budget is wasted, but I'm not sure which half"—is often true. Up to half of all advertising for established products is ineffective or only minimally effective. Perhaps no other industry has a failure rate as high as the advertising industry. It results from weak marketing know-how and faulty consumer feedback mech-

anisms. You can fix all of these by making your agency people go
to consumers before your advertising goes into production.

Manufacturers think they have found an alternative to ineffective advertising. They're increasingly cutting advertising and
increasing promotion. But promotion is for short-term growth.
Advertising is for the longer term. Promotion can help a company grow, but advertising will build it.

To-the-Heart Advertising Creates
Goodwill in Surprising Places

Advertising to the heart has a hidden advantage—not subliminal,
but hidden. As well as leading consumers to buy your product, it
shows your salespeople that you mean action. It placates distributors and ancillary groups. Liquor companies place billboards in
front of distributors' offices, even if the offices are in a bad part of
town (which they usually are). The ads are more about massaging
the distributor than about directly selling goods. The ads create a
warm "they care about me" feeling in the distributor's heart.

Ads from the Wool Bureau, a trade group to support the sale
of wool, are really more about pleasing sheep ranchers than
about selling goods. Most of its advertising to consumers is
wasted, and the Wool Bureau knows it. The advertising is a
hodgepodge of questionable physical benefits. For the sake of
pleasing its membership, the Wool Bureau has forgotten a cardinal rule of advertising: One strong benefit is more powerful than
a menu listing of smaller benefits. Too many benefits dilute a
strong selling message. Besides its warmth, which many syn-
thetics can now easily match, the consumer-perceived strength
of wool is in its endearing emotional qualities. I mention that
only because most associations like the Wool Bureau are bent
more on pleasing constituents than on selling to consumers.

The Difference Between Customers and You

Emotion sells. One of the real-world problems in creating emotional advertising is that copywriters are too smart, or at least

they think they are. They work in big towns like New York and Los Angeles, but the people who buy the advertised products live in places like Waukegan, Illinois, and Albuquerque, New Mexico. The sophistication level is different. Not better or worse, but different.

Product managers and higher-level management also have a different viewpoint from consumers. They know their product too well and reject emotional cues because they seem too simplistic. Consumers are simplistic—and I don't mean this in a bad way. They don't care about your product long enough to look for deep meanings in an ad or to translate your lofty symbolism:

> What you and your agency find corny, consumers will find touching.
> What you and your agency find trite, consumers will find art.
> What you and your agency find redundant, consumers will find sprightly and original.
> What you find powerful, consumers will find trite.

Talk to Consumers in Their Own Words About What's Troubling Them

Falling back on trade jargon is also a bad idea. It happens in trade advertising and in advertising for consumer goods. Speak in the language your customers speak.

When your ads mention that a product is shelf-stable, consumers will think it won't fall out of the pantry.

When your ads talk about a high-carbon forged steel drill bit, consumers are only looking for 3/4-inch holes.

When your ads talk about mouth feel, consumers will laugh or, worse, totally ignore the pitch. They just want a shot of some upscale-sounding vodka for their orange juice. Several years ago, Seagram's candidate for the Bad Advertising Hall of Fame was a series of ads about the mouth feel of its vodka. What is mouth feel, and who cares?

At times, your product is the most important thing in a consumer's life, even if it is mundane to you. Let's say someone is planning a dinner party. That person's needs are almost manic.

"What am I going to serve?"

"How am I going to make it?"

"What are my friends going to think of me?"

A sense of panic sets in—a panic that you can assuage with your product when you position your product as hero, ensuring that the dinner party will be successful.

Cascade dishwashing detergent has done a magnificent job over the years with its "sheeting action" that does away with water spots. Water spots are not on anyone's top ten list of societal ailments. Over the years, however, these commercials have made consumers downright paranoid about the little devils. Not because the water spots are bad, but because the host thinks they make her or him look slovenly.

Aristotle and Advertising

One doesn't often get to quote Aristotle in a marketing book (and thanks to Barry Golliday of Information Resources for pointing out the following). Even though advertising as we know it probably didn't exist back then, the basic communications elements were the same. One person was trying to persuade another. Aristotle pointed out three key elements necessary to persuade, in order of importance:

1. Credibility
2. Emotion
3. Rationality

Credibility Versus Believability

If one person tries to sway someone else toward buying something he or she makes or accept an idea he or she espouses, then that person must be credible. Credibility is a synonym for trust. An ad must be credible if it is to succeed.

There's a difference between credibility and believability in an ad. Managers and ad researchers (again misguided) test advertising premises to make sure they are believable. Believability is really not that important. Good advertisers know that consumers will suspend disbelief when an ad or product strikes a psychological nerve.

The creative person's job is to make consumers *want to believe*. Credibility provides them with that rationalization.

Wanting to believe is a vital part of advertising and marketing, and of life. Consumers are quite willing to suspend disbelief when you develop the proper to-the-heart ad. If you promise in your ad that a cream is going to eliminate wrinkles forever, some consumers will buy it in the hope that it will remove *some* wrinkles for a while. Maybe it will mask wrinkles just for the evening.

The scratch-off Lotto games are another example of the suspension of disbelief. People don't really believe they're going to win the hundred-thousand-dollar prizes, but when they win two or five dollars, the emotional positioning of an ad that says that they *can* win is reinforced. The fact that newspapers talk about big winners makes the claim credible. Psychologists actually have a term for this. It's called the intermittent reward. They did a study in which pigeons pecked at a door for food. The pigeons that were always provided with the food when they pecked at the door soon lost interest. But the pigeons who were given the food only intermittently never lost interest. They continued the activity in search of the reward.

That's the same kind of force that drives consumers to try your product when your advertising claims to fill some sort of need that consumers find important. Not all of the products they try work out, but just enough of them do. Not all products do what an ad claims they will, but some do. That's what keeps consumers coming back for more. In a business-to-business situation, your prospective customer may have tried all kinds of vendors. Some performed well, some didn't. The person may give you a chance because he or she thinks that you may work out.

Consumers may not rationally believe your premise, but if your message and target audience have been properly selected, they will suspend disbelief and give your product a try.

Take Alpha Hydroxy skin care complex. The product is supposed to help you exfoliate (a hot-button word in the 1990s), moisturize, and keep you from getting wrinkles in the future. Sort of unbelievable, isn't it? But not to an Alpha Hydroxy customer. Here's what one said:

> It's worth a try. Suppose it *does* work. What if everyone buys it and uses it. Then their skin could look great (in a decade

or so) and I'll look terrible. I have Alpha Hydroxy everything now.

You're not misleading consumers in your advertising (but
then again, maybe you are), you're selling hope. Hope is a won-
drous thing. Without hope there would be no reason to go on
with life—no conquering impossible challenges. The smart
advertiser sells hope with a passion.

Emotional Appeal

Giving your product an emotional appeal is the quickest and
simplest way to cause consumers to suspend disbelief. We said in
an earlier chapter that with an impulse item, all rational decision-
making processes are short-circuited. It's up to the advertiser to
alter consumer perception so that the emotional premise you set
out in an ad is so strong that it carries through to the purchase situation. Since the power of emotional appeal is the underlying
theme of this whole book, I need not belabor the point here.

Rational Appeal

Of all the appeals to consumers, rational appeal is the weakest.
It is the hardest appeal to get across in a print ad or thirty-second
commercial. Moreover, educating consumers about the rational
usefulness of your product is expensive. You must develop
strong reason-why copy and repeat your message many times,
until consumers finally say, "Yeah, that makes sense."

When you have an emotional appeal, you sometimes need
to back it up with a quick rationale. For a relatively inexpensive
product, if you need a rationale at all (and you usually don't), it
shouldn't take more than a phrase or two at most. Consumers
don't care how the product works as long as it reinforces the
product benefit claim.

If your product is relatively expensive, or if the product
must appeal to both influencers and buyers, the rationale should
be somewhat more extensive. Swimming pools are usually purchased by men, yet the woman in the household is the initiator
or the key influencer. You must arm the woman with a rationalization so that she can sell the idea to her spouse.

Even if there is no spouse to persuade, for an expensive product, a clear reason why is usually necessary (along with the emotional pitch) so that one side of the consumer's brain can persuade the other side to go along with the purchase. For an expensive product, the buyer sometimes has to sell him- or herself, and that can be the hardest sell of all.

In a business-to-business situation, in addition to your wonderful personality, you're going to have to present backup rational benefits so that your product or service can be sold to all the links in the purchasing chain of command.

The Plot Thickens: How to Connect With Your Customers

Did you know that in all of literature, there are only thirty-six plots? That's taking into account the works of Shakespeare and every other celebrated writer. Every work of literature is actually a variation on one of these themes, whether the variation is a character enhancement or changes in the plot specifics.

I mention this because it's related to the creative product. Copywriters claim to feel hemmed in if limitations are placed on their work, and they detest having to follow a formula. But if all of world literature can be boiled down to thirty-six plots, surely we can find a creative way to sell your product. Even if we include these set-in-stone basics:

▷ *Target* your customer.

▷ *State* the customer's problem and/or possible motives and communicate your emotional benefit.

▷ *Solve* the problem. If there is no specific problem, (e.g., if you are selling a new soft drink), show how the product satisfies a need or want in a new way. At the very least, sell the product in a way that consumers can identify with—a way that's important to them. It sounds easy, but most creative people want their ads to be "different." Being different is great, but missing the mark because of being trendy is a waste of the client's money. (Check out the commercial discussed in Chapter 3 again.)

▷ *Drive* home the name of the product as often as you can. It's trendy today to mention the name of the client's product only at the back end of the commercial. Sometimes this works, but not usually—not anymore. Consumers have seen the technique so often that they have become inured to it. It's no longer as intrusive as it once was. One of the most emotional (non-public service) commercials of the early 1990s was for a home pregnancy test kit. The cameras watched while two people awaited the results. There was pathos, suspense, warmth in this beautiful thirty-second spot. Too bad the brand name was lost. Failure to register your brand name is one of the most common weaknesses of commercials. Next time you review your advertising, make sure your brand name is clearly stated and shown and that it registers with your customers.

You don't have to make your points in that order, but all of them should be in every ad. This does not preclude creativity. In fact, it sharpens the creative product. It makes your commercials and ads more focused because you are writing a "personal message" to a unique audience that more willingly accepts your message.

It's great to be entertaining—you'll get noticed—but there has to be something concrete behind the entertainment. You can even make a case for the banal being effective. In the 1960s, there was a totally obnoxious commercial for Kraft Foods' Shake 'N Bake chicken coating. A mother would put the breaded chicken on the table and a little girl, in a very false, saccharine southern accent, would say, "And I helped." The commercial was roundly lampooned. But it worked. It hit the hot button of family values, although they didn't call it that in those days. Thirty years later, Kraft has revived the commercial. It's still obnoxious. And it still works.

The Shake 'N Bake commercial was not liked by the majority of people, but it sold. A commercial does not have to be liked to be effective. One of the so-called tests of advertising is its likability quotient. This test is worthless. You're not out to please people, you're out to sell products. If your product is no good, your customer isn't going to like you anyway, so what's the difference? In your advertising research, don't ask people what they like, ask them what they remember.

Advertising agencies (particularly creative people) pride themselves on connecting with consumers. Paradoxically, most creative people are against research that puts them in touch with consumers—"I know what's right" is the attitude. "Don't confuse me with the facts." Great production values will enable a creative director to develop a well-crafted, interesting commercial, but they won't enable that person to empathize with your prospective customer. An interesting graphic or sound bite has a long way to go before it presents a cogent benefit to consumers. It's not how cool your computerized multimedia toys are, but how you use them. Weak advertising sells at consumers. Effective advertising empathizes with them.

Just because a commercial looks good from a design standpoint does not mean it is well thought out. Persuasiveness comes from the heart and plays to the heart. The message is not generated by cameras and sound crews, it is generated by a creative person who has looked into the heart of the consumer he or she is trying to sell to.

What should be created comes directly from consumers. It's like a real-world connect-the-dots game. Consumers will give you a bunch of insights based on emotional cues, and you have to connect the dots to create an ad that makes sense. Most of the time, consumers don't even know their own feelings. That's why the smart marketer uses strong reactive stimuli in focus groups or any kind of consumer interview. If consumers are not fully aware of their own feelings, why should someone writing copy in an enclosed cubbyhole in an office know what those feelings are?

Chrysler Dodge Neon connected by laying out its good points in an entertaining manner and letting its young target audience make their own decisions. The visual was simple: car and background. The advertising was straight to the point (the graphics were strong, but they didn't dilute the selling message): "I'm now an adult and I can choose the car I want."

Even the best advertising won't move a product if the product doesn't make an emotional connection to someone or resolve real consumer needs. As mentioned in Chapter 6, and as the people who put milk into those little juice boxes know, it's difficult to educate consumers. Those boxes that don't need refrigeration have been sold in Europe for a long time. They haven't sold here. The reason is simple: Refrigerators have been invented. We had refrigerators in our homes long before Europeans did. The boxes are totally contrary to our belief that milk and most food products that are not in a can are perishable.

Advertise to where consumers are *now*. It's expensive to reeducate consumers. We all know that we shouldn't put metal in a microwave. Right? Wrong. Most of the new microwaves have eliminated the problems of sparks and arcing. But consumers are still afraid. It's better to advertise to what consumers know now, rather than try to change an opinion.

Other Forms of Advertising That Work

There is a tendency to talk about advertising as if it included only paid media. That's only one form. Everything you present to your prospective buyer is advertising because it reflects on your credibility and the good feelings you provide.

Lifesavers was recently changed to a bigger roll. Said the brand manager, "We wanted to find a way to show people that value—getting more for your money—still exists. We decided that the best way to do this was to add more candy to the rolls."

Frieda's Produce, a distributor of vegetables, uses point-of-purchase material extensively. Each individual item is labeled with Frieda's name along with the name of the product, suggested uses, and recipes.

One of the guiding philosophies at Frieda's is that food is more than sustenance. Food is fashion, and the wants of consumers constantly change, and so Frieda's products and promotions reflect that change.

Different types of restaurant cuisine come into and go out of style. Southwestern used to be popular, then it was Caribbean food. Produce departments are often unable to keep up with the most current trends. Frieda's point-of-purchase advertising and recipes help the store and consumers keep up with changing tastes.

Packaging: Your Sell in the Store

In the 1990s, packaging is also an ad vehicle—as vital as what's inside. Your package has to sell, sell, sell. You have only a few brief seconds to capture consumers with your package, so you'd better make the most of it. Creating an effective package requires cooperation between marketing and design. Instead, the conversation often goes like this:

Designer (after numbing the brand manager with 100 package mockups and narrating the alleged creative story behind each of them): So which one do you like?

Manager: They are all off strategy, but I guess I like number seventy-nine if you can get my logo in.

Designer: There was no room for the logo.

Manager (trying to be diplomatic): But management will really be upset if you don't have our logo.

Designer: I'll try to put it in on our next round.

That really happened!

Efficiency is the name of the game when it comes to something as vital as your package. You have no space to waste. The front of the package is the headline; the package back is the reinforcement. The side panels also play an integral part by further reinforcing the emotional selling message.

Now I'm going to get in trouble with the package designers, but the package is no place for subtlety. It should grab consumers by the throat and shout, "Buy me."

Good packaging cajoles, invites, and persuades your customers to grab the package from the shelf and take it home. It has to work harder today because the helpful in-store salesperson has gone the way of real whipped cream—meaning you hardly see it anymore. Your package has taken the salesperson's role.

A good package differentiates your product from every other product. It sets your parity product apart from the also-rans. It can also transform a loser into a winner.

Good packaging functions as a headline on the shelf. It reeks of consumer benefit. It has as much visibility as the Goodyear blimp. The results of good packaging are speedy trial and a positive feeling about your product. Good packaging grabs the consumer like the hook at the old-time vaudeville theaters. Eventually you're going to stop couponing and commercials. Your product is going to have to sell itself . . . naked to the world.

A creative package reaches out to consumers so that they reach out for the product, almost without realizing it. A good package front prospects for consumers and invites them to learn more about the product from the package back.

A good package conjures up in consumers' minds clear images of what the product is going to do. Even though food never looks as good as it does on the package, consumers usually want a food shot on a food product. Food usually tastes better when it's enjoyed in a restaurant with a fancy name. Restaurateurs know that presentation of your dinner is a major contributor to the success of the meal. And your package is your presentation.

The best packaging and advertising promise security and empathize with the target consumers' life experiences. But don't overpromise and underperform. Fantasy is an illusion, but a margarine called I Can't Believe It's Not Butter or Move Over Butter had better taste like butter.

Tips for Making Your Advertising Work

Do do your research personally. *Don't* trust your research to housewives bearing clipboards at the local mall. It's not that these people are bad people, it's that they're interested in getting a quota of bodies and going home for the day. You're interested in learning about the subtleties of human behavior that will eventually drive your product.

Do hang out at a retail store. Watch how customers read labels and make buying decisions. Ask the buyers questions about why they bought the product. Treat the store as a laboratory of consumer behavior and marketing achievements. Learn about your customers by talking to them. Learn how they speak and, importantly, how they respond. Talk to them! It's a lot cheaper than getting a researcher to talk to them.

Do interactive groups—or create your own. If you can't afford a moderator, moderate them yourself. It's not rocket science. Show concepts, and watch how people react. If you can't afford a traditional focus group, be creative. For instance, if you have ads for a product for kids, go to a local nursery school for sampling, or to local little league or soccer games.

Do a communications check with people you *don't* know to make sure people are seeing the same thing you're seeing.

Don't ask consumers what they like. Ask what they remember. They'll almost always point to the emotional distinction that touches their lives.

Don't ask consumers what they like. Ask them what they'll buy.

Don't ask consumers what they like. Show them real-world alternatives and let them react. Don't show consumers hastily done concept boards. Show real ads. And show them a quantity—three or four ads hardly run the gamut of hot buttons.

If you can't afford groups, buttonhole strangers with ads. A major caveat: *Don't* ask a friend or a colleague what he or she thinks. The person will either be polite and tell you it's a nice idea or be brutal and say, "This is the stupidest thing I've ever seen." When you have a business product, talk to businesspeople in your industry. Most entrepreneurs don't believe that busy people will give up their time, gratis. They're wrong. Businesspeople are the easiest people to approach. If they know you're not trying to sell them something, they're usually thrilled to spend an hour or more talking about your product. People love to give advice and promote themselves as experts so that they can feel important (another hot button).

Tell Your Product Story

There have been many tomes written about advertising. With cumulative budgets running into the billions of dollars, it's fascinating to think that most advertising can be considered little more than expensive experiments. Maybe your approach is right, maybe it's wrong—but it can always be made better. To change advertising from the theoretical to the practical, test your ideas with consumers and make sure you've developed your emotional hooks to the max.

Ad agencies have been besieged by change for some time. Perhaps consumers have become too diverse and complicated for the traditional agency to serve as the one-stop marketing shop.

The formula for great advertising is simplicity of imagery and a strong end-benefit promise to the prospective buyer. Advertising is your product story—magnificently told.

▶ *10*

Making Consumers Embrace Your Products and Brands

It was a milestone in marketing history. The concept drove women wild with expectation. Women of all types marched into the venues, first sheepishly, then with full confidence. They meant business.

Men who had formerly patronized women visitors now took the time to talk to them as equals. It was rough at first. Women had not been accustomed to being treated with much respect in the past, and they didn't expect to be treated well now—they simply didn't belong there.

Now, however, their presence was not only accepted, but openly desired. Their money was good—if not gold.

The venue was the car dealership, and the product being sold was the Saturn.

Saturn put forth a totally new marketing idea that became vital to building the brand.

It treated women as people.

This chapter talks about building killer brands and how Share of Heart can help a product stand in front of the consumer and shout, "Take me, I'm yours."

A brand is more than a bottle, a nameplate, or a fancy box. It is a provider of good feelings and emotions.

This may sound like a stretch when the consumer is choosing a can of peas or a feminine protection product, but is it? The proof is in supermarkets and department stores. Name brands outsell store brands by more than ten to one, even though most store brands now match the name-brand products in terms of quality. Many store brands are made by the same people who make the name brands.

When consumers stop by the supermarket to pick up a jar of spaghetti sauce and a pint of cottage cheese, they pass aisle after aisle of brands and brand names. Most shoppers don't decide exactly what to buy until they reach the shelves. In the brief seconds of the shopping experience, the brand becomes the ultimate selling vehicle. The brand is the product that consumers will ultimately select or ignore. That means that a great deal is riding on the brand and everything the brand stands for.

Brand images and the products we choose indicate our contentiousness and differences (American Spirit cigarettes) or our friendliness (Budweiser, Coca-Cola, Coleman camping equipment). Our choices announce how we want to stand in society—how we want to be perceived by others. A bitter war is being waged between the Macintosh and IBM-compatible computers—not only between the companies but between the users. A real schism has developed. Macintosh users feel that they have a creative machine and a superior system. As we IBM users know, Macintosh is really a dead issue, with not nearly enough software available. Macintosh users deserve not scorn, but pity.

A typical prospective Saturn owner sees herself as on the cutting edge. She is buying from a company that she perceives as socially aware. In this case, she transfers that awareness to her own car-buying plight: "Yes, Saturn does care about me." The Saturn is the alternative upscale vehicle. People like the way Saturn runs its business. Saturn employees and salespeople just seem like "nice people." The Saturn may be a great car, but put a Chevrolet or Ford logo on the product and it wouldn't seem so special. The Saturn has to perform, but its advertising and its sales groups have delivered such a powerful relationship message that the company has a little leeway. If there are problems with a particular Saturn, customers chalk it up as a minor mistake. Yet if a customer has problems with a Ford Escort, he or she blames "those morons in Michigan."

Nice to Have Versus Want to Have

Usually customers will say that they want to buy from a socially conscious company, but this rarely translates into sales the way it does for Saturn (although it can be a component part of your image). That's why you keep grilling consumers on their purchase preferences. It's *nice to* buy from a socially aware company, but that's just not motivating enough to most consumers. The key words there are *nice to*. *Nice to have* is insufficient motivation to purchase most products. You have to change those words to *must have*. People once thought it would be nice to connect to America Online—sort of fun. Then they became addicted to it. They didn't realize how important America Online had become until the system broke down for a few hours. America Online had become a "must-have."

Must-have products usually provide an excellent level of product reinforcement, but just as important, they place an emphasis on satisfying a hot-button need. Only when you combine product reinforcement with satisfying a hot button can you create anything approaching total brand satisfaction and a must-have product.

Once you've melded the two, is your marketing work done? No, because the market is always shifting. Even as you are reading this chapter, consumer tastes and markets are evolving.

Take the hot button of poverty of time and the desire to organize. Day Runner, a time-management system, jumped into the market lead with its "schedule-in-a-binder" paper system. People who thought themselves busy cherished the product. They felt it was just the thing they needed in order to juggle their work and professional lives. But then Japanese companies developed "schedule-in-a-pocket" electronic systems (called PDAs, or personal digital assistants) that became the next time-management toy. Day Runner was no longer in the must-have category. If the company had been continually scrutinizing its product line, it might have found this out and worked out a deal with a

PDA manufacturer to use its strong name on a line of PDAs. A Day Runner PDA might have returned the brand to must-have status.

Nike and Sony are examples of must-have brands. In downtown Chicago there stands an homage to the once-humble sneaker. It's called Niketown. And it attracts more visitors—purchasing customers—than the region's famous Museum of Science and Industry. Right next door is a Sony showroom with hundreds of Sony products and hands-on displays.

In selling your product, you have to make your point quickly. Neither consumers nor your selling outlets will give you the time to work your product magic slowly. You do this by making your product story terse and pithy. Someone once said that a successful businessperson is one who can tell his or her entire sales story on the back of a business card. Your brand should function as a business card, conveying all the worthy components of your product or service in a brief image. The business card for a PDA might say, "Time management in your pocket (and it's a cool toy)."

A brand should state its benefit in one pithy sentence through imagery, association, and hard facts (see Figure 10-1).

Let's talk about you for a second. You're the ultimate brand.

You've worked hard for your success. Perhaps you're climbing the corporate ladder. Maybe you've spent a morning trying to woo a potential client with a heartfelt pitch. You've just prepared a twelve-page résumé or fifty-page proposal and given the interview of your life. Everything that could be said was said.

So why are you so nervous?

Because chances are you're going to be summed up by your interviewers in one or two sentences. And, of course, your dress, your manner, and the gestalt of your presence is going to contribute to that one-sentence description.

Figure 10-1. The one-sentence solution.

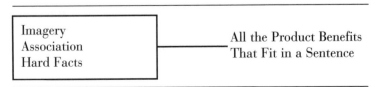

Yes, you are a brand. And you're hoping the interviewers will take a liking to you and buy you. If your whole life is going to be summed up like this, do you really think consumers are going to give a new soft drink any more attention?

Consumers Want to Be Sold

Consumers are always on the lookout for new brands and new products, so there are always new business opportunities. Yet consumers are always changing, so continuous evolution is the name of the game for brands and products.

But don't get too radical because consumers won't always accept a big change. They'll often think you've done something negative to an old brand, like taking out key ingredients or components. Let's be frank, sometimes you have. Marketers run the risk of losing their customers and their supporting retailers when they play around too much with the brand that brought them to the party. When you change things too much:

▷ Consumers don't know what they're buying (see the Coors example in Chapter 1).
▷ Consumers can't recognize the product because it's hard to find.
▷ Consumers think the product has changed, even when it hasn't.

Betty Crocker's Low-Fat Brownie Mix is an example of doing it right. The company gave the product a new name and package—and also put the older package on the front panel so that people who liked the product knew that it was the same product they had come to trust.

Make People Want You Because You're Special

Despite the advances in marketing techniques, many market segments are still dominated by the idea of selling the most products for the fewest dollars without any regard for to-the-heart imagery.

Commodity producers have long been controlled by brokers and wholesalers who are used to getting the product out at a fast and furious pace. Because of corporate downsizing, newly minted consultants work for bottom dollar. The real money comes from developing a brand (even if your product is a service) and making consumers buy your product because they feel a kinship to the brand. That's what Saturn did: It created an emotional link to car-buying females. It was a hook that had been missing for a century.

Even a product as simple as a mop merits consumer attention when it's marketed as something special. The Wondermop Company sold millions of dollars worth of its new "space age" mops, much to the chagrin of older mop companies who thought, "A mop is a mop is a mop."

Know What You Stand For

Back in Chapter 4, in the context of defining your mission statement, I asked, "What is your business?" An equally important question is, "What do your brand and products represent?" What is their significance—not to you, but to your customer? Kellogg's may think that it is selling frosted corn flakes, but it really may be selling Tony the Tiger. Nestlé has been selling its Quik chocolate mix for years. But its real strength is in the Quik bunny logo on the package.

These devices foster strong expectation in the minds of consumers. Tony the Tiger and the Quik bunny show that these products are going to be accepted by the children in the household—or even the baby boomer spouse. Even if it doesn't do anything else, the symbol should at least keep the kid quiet and satisfied for a few minutes.

When consumers make purchases, a number of things go through their minds. What you and your brand stand for is going to make a difference in whether or not they cross your name off the shopping list. The process actually starts before they enter the store, when they have a vague awareness of what brands will be offered and a preference for certain brands in a category. They wonder if they will have the money to purchase their first choice.

If money is an object, consumers might choose a store brand or a product they've heard of or had experience with. For a costly purchase, such as a stereo, they might wait for a salesperson's guidance. If it's a self-purchase or if the product is relatively inexpensive, they might try a new brand. The greatest likelihood of trying a new brand exists when all the brands on the shelf seem more or less identical and consumers want to add a bit of novelty to their lives or see what satisfactions a new brand can offer.

But whatever the circumstances, customers want to feel that they're making the right decision, even if the product is something as lowly as American cheese.

Marketing to the heart helps defeat the cynicism that is so rampant today. Trust in politicians, brands, products, and advertisers is breaking down. The power of the brand as trademark has been diminished for some people. Many consumers are saying, "What the heck, all brands are the same." So they count the slices in a package of cheese or tally up the sheets in a roll of toilet paper. But brands are not all the same when one offers an emotional benefit. It's a paradox. Along with a distrust of authority, consumers are gravitating toward premium brands with substance in a way they never have before. The more emotion a person has vested in a product or service, the harder it will be for that person to shift brands, and the less he or she will count paper towels and measure sheet sizes.

Hershey, Nestlé and Slim Fast have all recently issued scaled-down sizes of famous candy bars—and they're charging consumers more than ever. It's because of Share of Heart. They're offering a midday guilt-free self-reward of a chocolate treat with less fat than leading candy bars. Giving less and earning more—it's a wonderful concept when you do it right, by adding Share of Heart.

Know Your Influencers to Increase Your Selling Chances

Many purchases are made not for ourselves but for someone else. The purchaser wants this someone else to be happy with the product—or else the purchaser looks bad or, worse, faces a scowling significant other. The person who shops often has to account for

180 Marketing Straight to the Heart

his or her purchases to someone else. He or she is usually trying to please someone. Knowing your product means knowing the purchaser and the ultimate user of the product—and also the key influencer. Developing a brand image requires that you be honest with yourself. You can't fall in love with your product or its imagery. You have to please a great many people besides yourself.

Here's a scenario.

Purchaser: Here, kid. I bought you Cap'n Crunch.

Kid: I love Cap'n Crunch.

Significant other to purchaser: Why did you buy Cap'n Crunch? It's loaded with sugar.

Purchaser: He likes Cap'n Crunch.

Significant other: Only because you got him used to those sweet cereals.

Purchaser: Then from now on, you do the shopping.

As mentioned earlier, even a product as mundane as storage bags requires the approval of someone other than the buyer. For the Glad-Lock project, I watched as women in focus groups initially voted down the idea of the bags partly because they couldn't justify the added expense to their husbands. It was only when we created the positioning of "the bags that are so simple, even busy husbands and on-the-go kids can close them right" that they were able to justify the expense. They perceived that through the gimmick of the changing-color seal, they would actually gain their husbands' approval—or at least have an easy sell in the household.

Rarely does shopping occur in a void. The influencer could be:

▷ The purchaser and his or her conflicting emotions
▷ The kids
▷ The spouse or significant other
▷ Friends, including business associates
▷ Strangers
▷ The check-out store clerk

Don't laugh at this last one. There are personal products, such as incontinence products or condoms, that the purchaser can be embarrassed to take to the counter. This can actually erode sales. By buying a certain brand or product, shoppers are, in a way, disclosing their financial status and lifestyle to a total stranger. This can make a difference in sales.

In a business-to-business situation, the principle of pleasing people other than the actual purchaser works the same way. Only the cast of characters is different. You may think that a manager is trying to do his or her best for the company, but that is almost never the real priority. The buyers of your service want to make sure they won't look bad to their associates and bosses. Your brand should not only help the company, but enhance the prestige of the people who hire you. That is the most important part of a business-to-business connection. Position yourself or your product as the provider of a service that will make the buyer a hero. Of course, you can't say to the buyer, "I'm gonna make you a corporate god," but you can imply that you, as a brand, are going to make the buyer something special to management and peers. You can reinforce this message through your written and oral communication and the quality of your work.

Determine Your Imagery and Shout It

Not knowing your Share of Heart can be financially disastrous. Cadillac tried to attract a younger market with new car names like Allante and Cimarron, but younger consumers didn't see themselves as driving any car made by Cadillac (and I leave it to you to tell me why Cadillac thought those names would be appealing to younger consumers).

Imagery is of the utmost importance to brands, yet much of what is put on the package misses the target, creates a confusing or misleading message, or goes after the wrong audience, as Cadillac found out. These compromise choices are called conference room winners. Everyone in the conference room "contributes" something—a new name, a new product feature—but these do nothing for the consumer. When you have a product that has more features than consumers want, they will feel that they're paying for useless frippery and get resentful.

Specialize Specialize Specialize

Your product should do one thing and do it well. It should hone in on the image your customers have of themselves. Elements to optimize include your product benefits, your packaging, your pricing, and even the instructions. Don't be afraid to break hard-and-fast rules. There are few. The key commandment is to show your customers that they're making the right choice.

You can change your brand image, but it's expensive.

▷ It's easier to build a brand right from the start than to change consumer perceptions in midstream.
▷ It's more efficient to deal with the brand equities you have and satisfy your current customer base than to change your target market.
▷ It's more profitable to add incremental sales than to dis-illusion your current customers.

Brand Taxonomy

Here's a cognitive exercise that will help you create the imagery for your product and rule out superfluous or negative imagery (see Figure 10-2). I call it brand taxonomy—sorting your brand into brand image categories. Feel free to substitute the word *product* for *brand*.

Imagine your customer's lifestyle. Think of your customer as wearing a brand name pin on his or her lapel. This way of thinking is the inverse of the classic focus group question, "If the brand was a famous person, who would it be?"

Turn the question around. "If your target consumer was a brand, what brand would he or she be?" For instance, you may think of yourself as a "salt of the earth" personality, more concerned with basic performance than with flash. Your car brand preference may be a Chevrolet or Ford. You may buy Breyers ice cream and be perfectly happy with a utilitarian Bic pen. You disdain Lindt choco-late in favor of a Hershey bar. In other words, you are consistent in choosing brands with imagery that is similar to your personality. If you wore a lapel pin, it would say Arm & Hammer.

Suppose your target market was athletic, went to health clubs regularly, and was also in charge of a family. That con-

Figure 10-2. Brand Taxonomy—a cognitive exercise.

Imagine your customer's lifestyle:

> Adventurish
> Free Thinker
> Nature Lover

Brands this person chooses are:

> Isuzu Trooper
> Tom's Natural Toothpaste

Choose the imagery from their advertising and promotion

> Your prospective imagery goes here.

Does your imagery fit in and stand out?

sumer might identify himself or herself as an Isuzu Trooper. Choose your product's imagery from brands and products that have imagery similar to the Isuzu. The profile might be adventurous, youthful, willing to take chances.

Now select products or product areas that offer the same intangibles, such as sports drinks, energy brands of cereal, or athletic gear. Choose the imagery that is most successful within the category. Now build on it. What are these companies doing that is making their product so special to this market? How can you better this imagery so that your product will not only fit in but stand out?

But don't stop there. Build on it through consumer research to make sure your imagery is truly compelling.

Off With Your Brand's (or Product's) Head

You can also give yourself the quick death test, as in Chapter 6.
This product died because . . .

▷ It didn't keep up with the times.
▷ The benefit didn't fit the imagery.
▷ It offered no consumer appeal that merited a higher price.

Day Runner died (or got sick) because the new PDAs were perceived as faster and less cumbersome to carry around than loose-leaf binders.

Or, "Bic died because people were switching to upscale pens with snob appeal." Bic didn't die. It is doing quite well, but a simple test like this can show the company where it may be lacking. Perhaps it needs further line extensions to keep the brand vital.

Don't wait until your product actually dies to do this. If you can't think of a reason your product can die, you aren't being honest with yourself.

Be Specific

Both these exercises will give you an objective view of how your imagery and product fit into the lives of consumers and whether there is a key difference between your brand imagery and that of competing brands.

The closer, physically, your product is to the competition, the more you have to play head games with the consumer by creating a perceptual point of difference in the consumer's mind. Polaner jellies and Sorrell Ridge preserves went head to head against Smucker's with a natural, no-sugar-added positioning, a quality positioning that Smucker's itself defined years ago. Smucker's is attempting to win back its turf with a similar strategy. Not surprisingly, neither Polaner, Sorrell Ridge, nor certain varieties of Smucker's use the word *jam* or *jelly* on the jar.

Curiosity Drives New Brands and Products

When a consumer chooses a new brand, curiosity drives the purchase. After your brand has been used several times, consumers may get bored and switch to a newcomer in the category just for curiosity's sake. Or sometimes a product becomes so familiar that consumers actually don't see it anymore—as when you lose your keys and find that they've been staring you in the face. There will be newcomers as soon as the competition sees that your brand or product is a success. That's why you must keep fine-tuning your imagery and your product. You should be working on new enhancements to your brand or product even before it hits the market. Keep things lively to keep the consumer interested.

Competition will ensure that a better product than yours will be created. When consumers switch to a new brand, the brand they switch to becomes the one to imitate. But, of course, you have to make your product better.

Instilling Your Brands With Emotion Through Line Extensions

An effective line extension sells your entire brand while it sells itself.

It's a paradox that the same marketers who moan about the lack of brand loyalty keep groping after new line extensions. Nescafe has had so many line extensions, who knows what it stands for? ConAgra had phenomenal success with Healthy Choice. Then it extended the line into almost every food aisle, with soups, cereals, cold cuts, and more. It diluted the image so completely that Healthy Choice is losing share even in its flag-ship products, frozen dinner entrées.

On the plus side, there is the Crayola company. Once it made only crayons. Now it has leveraged its equity into more stores and markets with well-targeted line extensions. Crayola is not just a crayon company, but an art company—tools for the creative outlet.

Mailboxes Etc, a chain of stores that specialize in mailbox rentals, has made itself more valuable by adding new services that are important to home businesses. In addition to renting mailboxes, the stores have become copy centers and one-stop shipping centers. They wrap and box packages and have formed alliances with the major overnight delivery services. They have become "must stop there" shops.

Rubbermaid has always done a remarkable job of keeping its name vital and in front of consumers. It has products to organize everything. Now it's successfully branching into products for businesses.

Some Tips to Make Your Customers Love You

▷ *Give your brand a leadership position in a category or benefit area.* For instance, you can develop a leadership position as a budget brand or a high-priced brand. Be number one at something. The essence of positioning is to own an emotional or physical benefit and defend it aggressively.

▷ *One way of developing new brands is to name the competition in your advertising and promotions.* Then beat them at one aspect that is important to consumers. You should do this only if you are a second- or third-tier player. While you usually won't be able to bump off the leader, you'll create a frame of reference for consumers. They'll see you as a "leading brand" and everyone else as "others." However, your match-up has to be credible. If you're selling a low-budget car like the Ford Escort, it's foolish to compare yourself to a Mercedes. It's important that you realize that when you name the competition in your communications, you're also advertising the competition.

▷ *Infomercials, once the junk mail of TV, are a great way to learn the emotions that can drive a product.* As a rule, infomercials are highly researched. The consumer feedback is the sales they generate through 800 numbers. These sales are monitored every day. Just as in our interactive groups (groups are cheaper than infomercials), the producers keep what works and throw out or improve what doesn't. They are always testing new pitches and ideas.

Products are now filtering down to the "legitimate" distribution channels. Learn the techniques infomercial producers use. If you're looking for a new product, just knock off the products featured in the most successful infomercials. You can tell who's successful when you see a particular infomercial so much you're almost ready to buy the product.

Look at how sales are driven by emotion and backed up by a rationale. Notice how excited the studio audience is. People give the Wondermop standing ovations. Enthusiasm is contagious—and infomercial producers milk this excitement and transfer it to the viewer. (In case you were wondering, almost everybody in the studio audience is paid about $200 to sit and act excited. In our consumer society, if you can fake sincerity, you've got it made.)

▷ *Get your product into the consumer's hands physically, not just metaphorically.* When a person holds something, he or she is partly sold. That's why trinket and clothes vendors in tourist areas try to get the product into your hands. One person physically dressed my wife in a sarong right on the beach! She bought the sarong.

You can make consumers touch your product by using special textures on the package or making it an unusual shape. Such packages are more likely to be picked up than simple rectangular boxes.

▷ *Localize your brand.* Put a nearby geographical location on your product. People like to buy from people in their neighborhood.

▷ *Switch a brand from one category to another.* This is really more a cure for a stagnant brand than a technique for one whose sales are on the upswing. Changing your brand's category may lead to an upswing in sales. A cosmetics company developed a special kind of eye makeup for contact lenses. In the store, the makeup was placed with contact lens products. It failed miserably, for a simple reason: People wanted to buy their eye makeup in the cosmetic section. They didn't even think of looking for it in the contact lens section. Now there are complete lines of eye makeup that "happen" to be good for contact lens wearers—all of which are categorized as cosmetics rather than contact lens needs.

▷ *State the obvious, but do it in a new way.* If you have a new scent, don't say, "New scent." Say it in a way nobody has before. "Great linen scent" says freshness in a way that consumers can recognize and identify with. It's unimportant whether there really is a special linen scent. Consumers think there is such an aroma, and if consumers believe it, it's so.

▷ *State the rational need and the emotional need the product satisfies in a sentence or less.* The trick to a strong emotional sell is, to paraphrase *The New York Times*, "all the good feelings that fit in a sentence."

▷ *Sell the benefit, not the features.* Don't sell Bibles, sell salvation. Stress how the product can make consumers do something faster, better, or with more panache. If you're selling a convenience product, stress its quality, not its speed.

▷ *Align yourself both figuratively and literally with other brands that share your particular brand profile.* Create joint promotions for your brands and others so that the interest in both brands creates a synergy.

▷ *Deliver more then you promise.* It's a bonus. Consumers love to be surprised in a good way. Give them something extra—more product, more uses. Try giving thirteen of an item even though you say twelve on the package. When the consumer finds the thirteenth, he or she will think even better of you. A neat trick is to call attention to the thirteenth after the consumer opens the package.

▷ *Don't forget what brought you to the party, and don't improve your product to death.* It's natural to try to broaden your consumer horizons with a positioning that takes in a greater audience or to keep on improving your brand. But make sure your improvements hone in on the consumer's actual wants and need. Consumers won't buy more features than they think they can afford.

▷ *Determine your brand equity through interactive groups.* Constantly keep tabs on your equity by creating ads for your products with new positionings and new brand images and see if they improve on how you sell your product. Put your brand name on your competitors' ads and see if your brand name works better with your competitors' positioning.

▷ *In a business-to-business pitch, tell your customers you're going to write a proposal.* Then do it. (Who's going to say no to something that's free?) A proposal:

   —Gets the buyer to react (just as in interactive groups) so
      that you can respond favorably.
   —Keeps the relationship moving.
   —Creates expectations and excitement.

An added tip: When you write a proposal, make sure you include your prospective client's name in the contents as many times as possible. You can also turn the proposal into a personal letter. It's more effective than a boilerplate proposal.

Build Your Image

A brand image is your claim to fame. It's what makes your customers buy your product and continue to buy your product. The difference between a gimmick and satisfying a perceived consumer need is often simply salesmanship. The key is to be the best at something that's important to consumers and to keep building on your equities.

▶ *11*

About Value

In New York, one of the hottest businesses is day care centers—for dogs. People are paying from ten to thirty dollars to have someone pamper their pups in much the same way as kids attend day care centers. To many people, it's a value.

The person who invented sushi was a marketing genius. Sushi restaurants charge five dollars for a 1- by 2-inch sliver of raw fish served on a tiny section of rice. To many people, it's a value.

When a person pays $250 a month for five years for a car, $20 a month for the added control that a cellular phone provides is a value.

This book ends the way many books do: The protagonists fall in love . . . in this case with your product. Hopefully, the ideas you got out of this book were worth the small investment in cost. Actually *small* is a relative term—and that's the point of this chapter. Value is in the eyes of consumers, not marketers. In fact, *value* is a word consumers rarely use, unless they're filling out one of those ubiquitous, inane market surveys issued by clipboard-carrying people in the local mall.

The real question consumers ask is, "Is it worth the price?" The price is not always money. The price one pays for a product may be the time spent using the product. Our space program requires us to define values and emotion. Do we want to use our rockets and shuttles as transportation, or do we place more value on learning about our universe? Is it more important to put a man on Mars, or should we use the funds to go into the more distant heavens without a human on board? Is exploring the heavens worth the cost of even one human life—especially if we're not going to get any financial return? It's a question of value—and personal values. The emotionality of achieving a goal is what really put men on the moon.

Everyday Wants and Needs

Most decisions are not as momentous as deciding what to do about the universe. Most decisions are closer to home. They focus on the daily process of living and making life a little bit better.

A true value should offer consumers something dear to their hearts. Consumers know that value is more than just a low price, or simply adding one more ounce to a box of laundry detergent. Long after the price is forgotten, the consumer's feeling about your product's effectiveness will remain. If this book didn't meet your expectations, long after the cost is forgotten, you'll rue the time you spent reading it. But if you got one salient tip from it, it will have been a great value.

Eight dollars is a lot to pay for a movie if the movie is bad. Even more important than the money is the waste of an evening. The same eight-dollar movie is a bargain when it takes us out of ourselves and makes us feel excited, moved, or in some other way emotionally involved. Then, and only then, does it become what marketers call a value.

We can throw away a few dollars on lottery tickets and not mutter more than a quiet "damn" when we lose. But when consumers lay out $4 or $400 for a product, if it doesn't give them what they want, they'll never buy the product again. Consumers don't want to play product lottery. When they buy products, they want to win all the time.

A major company has tried to build a business by buying brands at bargain prices. When it gets a brand, it immediately cuts back on the active ingredients to strengthen the balance sheet—hardly a value. You can't scrimp on quality to save a customer money. People remember a product that didn't work far better than one that did.

In a recent survey by the M/A/R/C group, consumers were asked to compare store brands to national brands on five attributes: quality, selection, packaging, price/value, and trust. On all but the third trait, a majority of consumers considered store brands equal to or better than national brand alternatives. So why do national brands considerably outpace store brands? Because national brands have built up emotional links to consumers that are impossible to ignore.

Perceived Value Affects All Businesses

Most people don't stay with a particular health club because of all the flashy equipment the club has or the low dues. They are more interested in the people who work there. They want a friendly and helpful staff who will assist them achieve their goals.

When people buy products, they expect those products to be satisfying. When the products aren't, they're interested in how fast the problem can be fixed. People will usually buy the product again if the company shows a real interest in their total satisfaction.

A few days ago, I was in a wine store when a customer complained that a bottle of wine exploded in her car. The merchant's response was, "It's your fault—a hot car can do that." That store lost a customer. The woman vowed she would never return. The merchant should have replaced the bottle; the customer would have come back time and time again because of the goodwill that the store created.

Another Reason Products Fail

If brands are so powerful, why is the new product failure rate, even for successful companies, still about 90 percent? Because manufacturers are failing to develop products that consumers feel are worth the price. The products are redundant. Been there. Done that. No value.

Why There Is No Such Thing as a Value Strategy

Quality and value. We've heard it time and time again. It looks great in marketing research reports, but just what does it mean? That the product isn't going to fall apart when you get it home? That the new accountant you hired isn't going to get you thrown in jail? The fact that your product works should be a given. The premise that you're offering consumers value should be a given—and it can be judged only by the buyers themselves. Quality and value should be the foundation for your multistory marketing empire, not an add-on. Anything less is actually fraudulent.

A college education now costs a minimum of $50,000 and can rise to more than $100,000. Is that a fraud? Is it time wasted? Hardly. It's the cost of admission to today's society. High-priced, yes. A value, yes. (But nobody can determine what a "quality education" really is.) A true value must offer consumers something special.

Marketers say, "It costs me X to make my product. How can consumers expect me to make it cheaper?"

Simple. They don't care. They don't care how much it costs you to make the product or what your distributor adds to the cost of the product. As long as consumers get something they want at the time of purchase, they're happy.

You can't create value by scrimping on quality and performance. In fact, you can't create value at all. Value isn't something you put in a product, it's what consumers take out of the product. And this varies, because of the inconsistencies of the human heart and mind. Inexpensive store-brand ice creams and pricey premium items rise at the same time. To consumers, little luxuries can be major values.

Consumers usually have a range of prices that they're willing to pay for a product. This range is based on past experience, lifestyle, and (most vexing to marketers) how they feel at a given moment. To someone waiting restlessly for a plane, a fifty-dollar steak dinner can be a great value. Yet the same person might go bonkers if the local supermarket upped the price of hamburger a dime a pound.

Generating value is what marketing to the heart is all about. Consumers who buy the Infiniti car swear that what they value is the Infiniti's engineering. But for many, the value they get is the ability to sneer at people in their Fords and Chevrolets.

Whatever value—positive or negative—consumers get out of a brand remains in their memory long after the price is forgotten.

Creating value involves more than just offering a low price, though for many consumers that certainly is an important factor. But many people are willing to pay more for a product that provides something extra for them personally. A certain aroma, extra richness, or a fancy package can be an added emotional value.

Value-*added* marketing can work if you remember that consumers buy more from the heart than from the head.

Value added is . . .

▷ A sensory reward
▷ Peace of mind
▷ Making a loved one happy
▷ Attaining a fantasy
▷ Achieving a goal
▷ Having positive emotions stirred
▷ Being awarded for achievements
▷ Being stimulated
▷ . . . in the details.

A Word From a Philosopher

The following paraphrase wasn't about marketers and Share of Heart—but, then again, maybe it was . . .

"The role of reason . . . and emotion. Let reason be your rudder, let emotion be your sails as you fare the seasons of life."

—Kahlil Gibran

A Final Word
From the Author

Thank you for reading *Marketing Straight to the Heart*. If you have any ideas for future editions, please contact me at:

Barry Feig's Center for Product Success
6200 Eubank, Suite 423
Sandia Mountains, New Mexico 87111

You can call me at (505)-237-9342.

My e-mail address is newmex@aol.com.

I look forward to hearing from you.

Index